GIVE ME A RING

This book is dedicated to my late father, Hal Denver, a great showman and a tough sonovabitch, who I loved to bits.

And to my friend, Shirley Parris, who showed the courage of a true World Champion in the face of pain and adversity. Like everyone who knew her, I miss her.

GIVE
ME A
RING

THE AUTOBIOGRAPHY OF STAR REFEREE MICKEY VANN

MICKEY VANN WITH RICHARD COOMBER

MAINSTREAM
PUBLISHING
EDINBURGH AND LONDON

First published in Great Britain in 2003 by
MAINSTREAM PUBLISHING COMPANY (EDINBURGH) LTD
7 Albany Street
Edinburgh EH1 3UG

ISBN 1 84018 690 9

A catalogue record for this book is available from the British Library

Typeset in Berkeley and Helvetica Narrow
Printed and bound in Great Britain by Mackays of Chatham

CONTENTS

INTRODUCTION

Leaving Cardiff behind me, I edged the sponsor's white Ford Sierra into the Monday morning traffic on the M4 and eased my foot to the floor. I slipped an Aaron Neville tape into the cassette player and sang along as the car effortlessly ate up the miles towards London. This was as good as it gets. Having watched the TV replays, I knew I was in trouble again but that was nothing new. Anyway, I was confident that my four-letter outburst had been justified and even the prospect of a bollocking wasn't going to spoil this moment. I had achieved my greatest ambition – I'd refereed the fight for the heavyweight championship of the world.

I've always enjoyed being in the spotlight and the confrontation between Lennox Lewis and Frank Bruno had put me in the full glare of it, during the build-up and the fight itself in the Arms Park, and now in the aftermath. As I've always said, better to be infamous than ignored.

From very early in my life it was clear to me I was a bit different from most people. Not many of the kids I met had a dad who was an international showbiz headliner, who once threw knives at the mother of a future prime minister. On top of that, my grandfather was the Penny Showman, travelling the country urging the public to roll up and look at the Elephant Man, John Chambers the Armless Carpenter, the Ugliest Woman in the World, or Ellis the Hangman. With uncles and aunts also involved in shows, circuses and fairgrounds, my family was certainly not run of the mill.

As a kid I nursed a belief deep inside me that, no matter what, I too would be famous one day. Admittedly I thought it would be as a trapeze artist in the sawdust ring of the circus rather than in the square ring of the fight game. I looked at Dad and wanted to be like him. And I hung on to that hope, even though there were long spells when it seemed Mickey Vann's meagre claim to fame would be as a journeyman pro boxer, a game 'body' who was willing to take on anyone, anywhere, even though it often resulted in a bad beating.

As I sped along the motorway in the gentle sunshine of early October, going over the 'Battle of Britain' in my mind, I spotted the exit sign for Datchet. On impulse I took the slip road and drove round to the village of Wraysbury. Dad had once dumped me there while he went off to the States to appear in some show or other, and I hadn't been back for about 40 years. Little had changed. The George pub, where Henry Cooper and Percy Lewis used to train, was still there. In fact the only difference I noticed was that they had knocked down the school I'd been to. That was sad. I would have liked to see it again. It was the one school I'd enjoyed among the dozens I'd hated. Wraysbury had been good for me.

I was only there for a year, but that was a long time for me to spend in one place at that stage of my life. Just up the road from Slough, Wraysbury was a quiet village – Heathrow was just a small aerodrome then – and it was there I first experienced the buzz you get from success. I represented the county at gymnastics, athletics and football. I was champion boxer at school, and a member of the Bob and Ada Unsworth formation ballroom dance team. I was a bit of a somebody and I loved it, especially as I would miss religious instruction, music, metalwork and woodwork whenever Mr Basden, the games master, poked his head round the door and said: 'We need Mickey for training.'

As I wandered round the village, the memories came drifting back of how as a kid I'd slept in a lorry as we toured the country with the circus. Later I moved to Leeds, where I finally had a row with my dad and walked out. I was 14 years old, with no job and nowhere to stay. I grew up fast and soon learned to duck and dive, doing odd jobs that would bring in a few bob, and selling the trophies I'd won as an amateur boxer to help pay my way. I've never made much money but whenever I've been close to financial ruin, boxing has usually rescued me. I turned pro when I got married and was again desperate for cash to keep my young family. Ironically my wife hated all sport, especially boxing, and later she tried to sabotage my career as a referee just as I started to make a go of it. She got the hump because I constantly had a bag packed, waiting for the phone to ring, summoning me to another fight in another country. Needless to say, she became my ex-wife.

Inevitably that morning, at a time of great personal satisfaction, I thought of Karen, my girlfriend of five years. I wished she could have shared my greatest night, but that was a bit awkward because she was still married.

Above all, I thought of my dad and hoped he was proud that his son had taken charge of the world heavyweight title fight watched by millions all over the world.

ONE

The Bombs were the Easy Bit

I seemed to be trying to impress Dad all my life. I was never sure how he felt about me, right up to the last few days before he died. But I idolised him. Sure, there were plenty of times when I hated his guts, but I believe that, no matter how successful I am, I'll never achieve half as much as he did.

He was a master showman who went down a storm wherever he appeared, especially in the States, where he shared the bill with some of the biggest names of the time. He went over there a lot, working for MCA, one of the major entertainment companies, and there are contracts that show he was earning a thousand dollars a week back in the 1940s. I've got pictures and press cuttings of him with Errol Flynn, and working on the Ed Sullivan and Johnny Carson shows with people like Phil Silvers, William 'Hopalong Cassidy' Boyd, Mickey Rooney and Mamie Van Doren. He was also high up the bill at the Palace Theatre on Broadway. He was the tops.

Dad was only a small man, about 5 ft 6 in. tall, slim and wiry, but no one ignored him. He had a big presence that drew people to him but he could also be a hard bastard and could handle himself in a fight. People seemed to know instinctively not to mess with him. Everyone knew him by his stage name of Hal Denver, although he started life as Ralph Van Norman-Noakes. His act was spectacular. Some of the women in the audience would peep through their fingers as he sent 18-in. knives and hatchets flashing across the stage to thud into a board 24 ft away, each one landing scarily close to his partner's body. When I was growing up, his assistant was my second 'mum', Olga Frei, but according to some reports, earlier in his career he'd thrown knives at Gwen Major, the woman who later became the mother of the future prime minister, John Major. Apparently Dad's normal partner ran off to get married in the middle of a season and Gwen Major, who was in the same show with her husband Tom, agreed to take her place. In one of Dad's obituaries he was quoted as saying: 'The woman was a real professional and, although I've had three wives, there are only two ladies in my life I can think of with fond affection: my mother and a dear lady named Major.'

Show business was in Dad's blood. His father, Tom Norman, started life as a butcher's boy in Sussex but when he moved to London he got into freak shows and was known as 'The Silver King' and 'The Penny Showman'. He travelled the country and was often able to put on shows for nothing, thanks to the gullibility of estate agents. Pretending he wanted to look over a shop with a view to renting it, he would take the keys on a Friday night, install his freaks over the weekend, make his money and then shove the keys back though the agent's letterbox with a note saying the shop was unsuitable. I know it seems bizarre now that people would flock to pay a tanner to see Ellis the Hangman, the Lion-faced Woman, The Ugliest Woman in the World, or John Chambers the Armless Carpenter, but when you think about it there's not much difference in shows like *Big Brother*, which millions watch on TV. Grandad used to claim he had royal patrons, telling the tale that when Edward VII was Prince of Wales, he and some of his pals crept into the tent at Ascot to see Miss Eliza Jenkins, the Petrified Girl.

The most famous of Tom's exhibits was Joseph Meyrick, who became known around the world as the Elephant Man after the success of the film starring John Hurt. Social attitudes have changed a lot since then but even at the time there was a big stink about Grandad making a profit out of such deformity. People accused him and his partners of taking Meyrick out of the workhouse to exploit him, but Tom didn't see it that way. In a book of the old boy's memories, *The Penny Showman*, which my uncle George wrote and published privately, he wrote:

> The showing of Meyrick never appeared to any of us as being
> in any way detrimental to him – I mean painful. He was never

turned out of the workhouse – we made application to the proper authorities for his discharge, and after giving the guarantees required, we obtained his release after which he was not only in much better health but, as he frequently stated, much happier. He would never listen to the idea of returning to the workhouse . . . It is doubtless true that he never knew a parent's affection but I can honestly state that as far as his comfort was concerned whilst with us, no parent could have studied their child more than the four of us studied Joseph Meyrick.

I'm not sure how much comfort Grandad's idea of parenting would have been for poor old Joseph because, while my dad adored his mother and was always talking about her, whenever he mentioned his father it was in terms of how hard Tom made him work as a child. I guess that's where Dad got his ideas of how a father is supposed to act, because he too was a tough taskmaster and seldom showed his sons any affection or took much interest in what we were doing.

Dad's whole life was wrapped up in his work – right up to his death he was still appearing as an extra in soap operas like *Emmerdale*, and other popular TV programmes like *Vets' Life* and *Only Fools and Horses*. There's little doubt he was a very big name in his day. He'd performed in Lefty Clark's Sans Souci club in Havana alongside Edith Piaf, Tony Martin and Dorothy Dandridge, all major stars of the time, and he became friendly with the young Elvis Presley when they both appeared on the *Ed Sullivan Show*. The friendship grew at a family dinner shortly after the show. Before meeting Dad and becoming the target for his knives, Olga was an actress and took elocution lessons in Leeds from a woman named Pauline Hoare, who later moved to the States and married Elvis's uncle. She invited Dad and Olga to join her family and Elvis for a meal. The young singer was fascinated by Dad's chivs and spent most of the evening talking to him about his experiences around the world. You have to remember that in those days it took three weeks to get to America from Britain and people didn't travel anything like as much as they do today. Elvis was clearly impressed that Dad had been to places as varied as Switzerland, Holland, Russia, Germany, Canada and Mexico. They got on famously and Dad wanted to bring the budding pop legend back to England, but Elvis didn't think English audiences would take to him and turned down the chance.

America was where Dad made big money. Back home he ran shows and circuses, some with risqué striptease performances at a time when they were considered very wicked. The circus ran through the Norman veins. They were probably the biggest family in the business at that time. His brother George was the godson of legendary showman Phineas T. Barnum and also ran his own show. Together with another brother, Arthur, and a friend, Bert Fay, George formed a clown act, 'The Van Norman Brothers', and they toured the country for 30 years until Uncle George and his wife, Aunty Brenda, decided to retire to a shop in Clapham.

This was the world I was born into on 29 December 1943 in Camberwell, south London. I was christened Michael Van Norman. By then the Noakes had been dropped by all but a few relatives who thought they were a bit posh, and later I left off the Norman. Well, can you imagine a boxing announcer coming out with: 'In the red corner – Mickey Van Norman-Noakes!' Fighting was a hard enough game without a handle like that.

My mother was Ella May Knight, Dad's first wife and show partner. She was a sharpshooter and the sister of a well-known English 'cowboy' known as Rex Roper. She and Dad met when her father employed him for the Two-Gun Rix's show.

Dad had started to practise knife-throwing when he was 14. He was already working on the travelling fairgrounds run by his oldest brother, Tom. They were big business in those days and the gypsy lifestyle, with its hint of danger and glamour, was perfect for a wild-eyed kid with a restless streak. It was Dad's element and he was always upset when he was called back to Croydon from time to time to help out in his uncle Ralph's butcher's shop. Wherever he was, he would spend hours throwing knives, never tiring of seeing them flash through the air to their target, taking enormous pleasure from his increasingly inch-perfect accuracy. When he was in his early 20s he was good enough to form an act with his sister, my Aunty Nelly, who is now over 90 and living in Rugby with another sister, Aunty Amy, who is approaching 100. The Desmoines, as they called the act, found it tough to get work but they kept going and when Dad was 34, he landed a good job and found himself a wife.

It's pretty obvious that neither he nor Ella had any interest in becoming parents. Two years before I came into the world, my brother Monty was born and within ten days of taking his first breath, the baby was put with a foster family, the James's. I must have been a cute kid because I was six weeks old before I was shipped out to 258 Farley Road in Warlingham, Surrey. Later Dad claimed that Hitler's bombing made it too dangerous for me to stay with him and Mum. As a kid, I accepted his explanation but looking back it's got more holes in it than Frank Bruno's defence. Warlingham is not far from Biggin Hill, one of the key RAF stations during the war, and to try and fool the Germans, the government built a dummy aerodrome in the football field right behind our house. No wonder Farley Road was known as 'bomb alley'. All the rest of the kids in the street had been moved out; I was evacuated in. If that was to protect me, I wonder where Dad would have chosen to put me in danger? On one occasion an incendiary bomb hit the house and the fire brigade had to rescue us; on another the vicarage next door to us was bombed and I was found lying on the lawn having been flung out of my pram by the blast. You might ask why I had been left in the garden during a raid, but that was fairly typical of the care taken by Matey and Jamie James. I was with them six or seven years, and I hated every moment.

The James's fostered about six kids at a time. They took an instant shine to Monty and an even quicker dislike to me. I suppose I was a little sod, always falling out with Monty and being a bit wild, but I never felt they wanted me there. Matey was a tough old bird with ideas on bringing up kids that would probably see her prosecuted these days. If you marked your underpants, she would rub your nose in it then make you wash them. If you swore, you had to eat soap. I'm not kidding – she would soak a bar of Lifebuoy in the bath until it was soft, then make you eat it. I must have started swearing young because I seemed to eat a lot of soap and I only have to hear the word 'lifebuoy' now to taste it again and recall the sick feeling I had for hours afterwards. It never did stop me swearing.

Matey was a fierce-looking woman, probably aged about 60, with grey hair dragged back into a tight little bun. She had a sharp, pointy nose and round shoulders that made her look even shorter than her 5 ft. I always think of her in a flowery dress with the sleeves rolled up over her strong arms, a flowery apron, thick stockings and heavy black shoes. Jamie was a stocky fella with thinning hair. He always wore a V-neck jumper over his collar and tie, and inevitably grey trousers. He ran a taxi service in his black Wolsey but at home, she was the boss and he did what he was told. Every morning the pair of them would line us kids up so one could shove a dose of syrup of figs down us to keep our bowels moving, while the other administered a spoonful of malt to ward off colds and flu.

She and I were bound to come into direct conflict as soon as I was able to get around. She liked everything to be orderly and under control, for the children to do as they were told and to spend much of their time sitting still so as not to disrupt her routine. I guess I was what is talked about these days as hyperactive or as it was once described, having ants in my pants. I found it impossible to sit still, and as soon as she turned her back to attend to one of the other children, I'd shoot out through the back door to play. She got so fed up with this that she started to tie my legs to a chair. One day she got angrier than usual, grabbed me and strapped me to a chair in front of a mirror and told me to 'look closely, so you'll see what a horrid boy looks like'. If she thought she would upset or shame me, she was well off-beam. I just sat there pulling faces and grinning at myself. That ability to keep grinning has got me into and out of plenty of scrapes in my life.

Matey clearly had me marked down as a troublemaker because she always used to sit next to me at the meal table so she could give me a crack if I did something she didn't like, which seemed to happen quite often. Meals were taken around a large table that extended by opening up two ends and inserting a leaf in the centre. You had to eat in silence, clear your plate and stay still until everyone was finished, or she would take a spoon and whack you across the knuckles.

Her other favourite punishment was to send you to bed early. We'd get back from school and have tea about four o'clock, then we were allowed to race around the garden until half past five when, as one of the youngest, I was supposed to go to bed. But more often than not, I'd do something to upset her and I was off to bed straight after tea. I quickly turned that to my advantage because I used to creep around upstairs exploring. One day I sneaked into her bedroom and found a cupboard with shelves stacked with food, including chocolate bars. Pretty soon I was helping myself on a regular basis. I had to be careful because God knows what she would have done if she had caught me. I'd keep listening to the sounds downstairs and if the living-room door opened, I had to get back to the dormitory as quickly as I could without making a sound. I got to know that landing so well I could have got across it blindfold. I was aware of every squeak and groan of the floorboards – I used to count the squares on the carpet and knew which to avoid – and I could shut the bedroom door to within an inch of where it would make a noise and give me away. Once inside her room, I was quickly looking at neat piles of silver-and-pink squares inside which was mouth-watering, chocolate-covered coconut. Even at the age of five or six I knew better than to nick just one, because the gap in the piles would be obvious, so I used to shuffle things around to make it look as though the sweets hadn't been disturbed. There were times when she seemed suspicious and would search my pockets, but I used to hide the sweet papers in the toe of my shoe and throw them away when I walked to school. I never got caught.

Dad was away in America most of the time and would keep in touch with occasional letters. Monty and I would wait for the postman, always hoping he would be carrying one of those distinctive, blue airmail envelopes. About once every six months Ella would visit and take us to a local teashop in Warlingham, which was a huge treat. One year I missed out and Mum never did know why. The truth was that I was an hour late coming in one night and Matey James sent me straight upstairs to the dormitory. I was getting washed when she came up behind me and beat the back of my legs so hard I couldn't walk. I could hardly get out of bed. In order to go to the toilet I had to drag myself along the landing, hold myself up, and then drag my way back. When Ella came, they told her I was in bed with a sprained ankle. I was too scared to say anything, so Monty went off to tea on his own with a big grin on his face.

That was typical of Monty. There was little brotherly love between us. We seemed to want exactly the opposite in everything. That was especially true when it came to Dad. Monty hated him and everything to do with his way of life. In those days Warlingham was a small village with lots of woodland, and Monty thought of himself as a country boy.

He didn't want to know about towns, and especially disliked circuses and fairs. Probably the first time we really got to see more than a brief glimpse of Dad was when he came to take us with him to the circus one summer. I loved it. I could run around as much as I liked, no one kept telling me to wash behind my ears or to be quiet, I stayed up until half past seven and even later some nights. I was thrilled by the buzz of the circus, the fact that I always had little jobs to do, and above all, the fact that I was with Dad. Monty cried and moaned nearly the whole time. He wanted to go back to Warlingham almost as soon as we arrived, and from then on, if he heard Dad might be making one of his rare visits, he'd go and hide in the woods.

Like so many brothers, Monty and I were always falling out. He was always teasing me and, being small and feisty, I would respond violently and find myself in even more trouble. Dad used to send money for us from the States and Matey James decided Monty deserved to have a pedal car out of this cash. He spent hours in that car and wouldn't let me anywhere near it. I was seething but it didn't take long for me to get my revenge. One day he was standing next to the garden door, taunting me about his bloody car, so I slammed the door on his fingers. Another early night for Mickey. On another occasion he tapped me on the shoulder and when I turned round he was standing there, threatening to bring a hammer down on my head. When he finally let it fall it turned out to be rubber. He thought it was hilarious but by then I was so terrified and angry that I went off to the garage, got a real hammer and whacked Monty in the mouth, knocking out several teeth. That stopped him laughing.

Around that time Mum and Dad split up and she came to Warlingham to 'kidnap' Monty and me. She took us to her sister Jessie, who was a tattooist in Aldershot, catering for the servicemen in the area. We had a room at the back of the shop where we could lie in bed watching Jessie jabbing needles into her clients, creating garish pictures or messages of undying love to 'Mum', 'Brenda' or some other woman, on the biceps of squaddies who usually looked far too hard to be that sentimental. They were always so distracted by Jessie's artistic genius, or maybe it was the pain, that it was dead easy for me to go through their greatcoat pockets and nick a newspaper or a few cigarettes which I could later take round the corner and sell. In those days Players Weights, Woodbines and Senior Service were sold in packets of five, and some shops sold them individually, but I quickly learned to undercut them.

Most of the time I was free to wander wherever I liked and would go off for hours on end. It was on one of these jaunts that a soldier started to chat to me and I quite happily went off with him. It was only by chance that we bumped into Mum and Monty in the street and they took me home. Now I dread to think what he was after but at that age I had no idea there could be danger. No one told you not to talk to strangers back then.

Monty also went off a couple of times when he overheard Jessie say that Dad might be coming to pick us up. The first time they found him in Gloucester, the second time in Brighton. He must have been a gutsy kid, but that didn't register with me at the time. We were still falling out regularly. Builders had left some materials behind Jessie's house and one day Monty decided it would be fun to throw handfuls of sand in my face. Eventually I lost my rag, picked up a lump of brick and thumped him on the head. It was a couple of days before Christmas and when we woke up on the 25th, Santa had brought Monty a big grey battleship but nothing for me. He sat there, head bandaged, looking smug. I could quite cheerfully have whacked him with another brick.

Eventually the authorities tracked us down, decided that the backroom of a tattooist's shop wasn't the ideal home for two young kids and dragged us back to Warlingham. Naturally they didn't ask me what I thought, and I guess I accepted that was the way life was. The James's was the last place I wanted to be but at least I knew where the sweets were stashed. About this time Dad made one of his rare visits and for once Monty hadn't caught wind of it, so the three of us set off together for the Schoolboys Exhibition at Earls Court. As usual Dad was wearing his full-length Crombie coat with padded shoulders that made him look bigger. He was also sporting a fedora and as we arrived at Earls Court he stuck a press card in the hatband and, carrying a large camera, strutted through the entrance with us in his wake. We were in without paying.

That camera caused quite a stir because it was one of the first Polaroids seen in England. It had a big silvery dish for the flash and the front folded out like a concertina. When he took a picture, he pulled out the previous negative, pressed a button and counted 60 seconds under his breath. Then he'd open the back and pull out a black and white print with a neatly serrated edge. He'd wipe it with some wax and shake it until it dried, and the picture would be ready. I've still got a couple of those photos at home. Dad smuggled a load of cameras in from the States and we soon received a visit from the Customs and Excise, who rolled up in their Humber Snipes to turn our place over. They took away a few cameras, but Dad had already flogged some and stashed a few more with Aunty Brenda and Uncle George at their shop in Clapham.

After spending the afternoon at the exhibition, we got the tram back to stay the night at Dad's place in Brixton. Somewhere south of the river, the tram stopped at some traffic lights and Dad started to rap on the window to attract the attention of a blonde woman waiting to cross the road. 'See her?' he said. 'That's your mum.' I was a bit puzzled and thought: 'Blimey, last time I saw her she was a lot bigger than that and had black hair.' It was my first glimpse of Olga. By now Mum and Dad were divorced. A report in one of the papers read: 'Ella May Knight left court grim-faced with her lawyer by her side. Two minutes later Hal Denver came out with a blonde on his arm and a smile on his face.'

I enjoyed staying with Dad, but as soon as we were taken back to the James's things became pretty miserable again. I swear we had Shiphams meat paste for tea 365 days a year. Things came to a head one day when Monty and I were coming home from Sunday school. As usual, we'd fallen out and I was chasing after him to whack him. He rushed out from behind a bus and was hit by a car. I just legged it away from the accident and as soon as I got indoors, made out I didn't know where Monty was. I was upstairs when the police came to tell the James's he was in Purley hospital and I stayed out of the way that night, certain I would get the blame. Monty was laid up for 18 months and that was the final straw for Matey James. She said: 'We can't take care of both of you. We want to adopt Monty and your dad's coming for you.' I couldn't have been happier.

Dad rolled up to collect me in a seven and a half tonne, blue and grey, flat-faced Morris Commercial lorry which was to become my home. I can still remember the number plate – CRW 806. I was ready at the door for over an hour before he arrived, my few possessions – some clothes, a grey-and-red-striped school tie, and a lead soldier – in a cardboard suitcase. 'Where's the rest of your stuff?' Dad wanted to know. When I told him this was it, he stormed up the path and I heard him having a hell of a row with Matey James. With the money he'd been sending, he'd expected me to have boxes of toys and suitcases full of clothes. He went bananas at her. I bet she thought: 'Blimey, now we know where the little one gets his temper.' I've still got that tie and lead soldier at home today.

I didn't care how little I had. I was just happy to be living with Dad at last. We drove to 51 Blenheim Gardens in Brixton, right next to the jail. It was there that Dad kept his caravan. It was our winter quarters where we stayed when we weren't on the road. He was always happiest living in a caravan. Even when he bought a mansion in Garforth, he parked the van in the grounds and ran a cable into the house for his electricity. In Brixton, my sleeping quarters were in CRW 806. You got in the driver's side and climbed over the seat to a little doorway, behind which was a bunk. I loved it – it was like camping every night.

The next day we went out with the circus. Dad loaded an old Maudsley coach with props, the canvasses were piled on my lorry, and off we went round the country. This was perfect. So you can imagine how I felt when one Saturday as we were loading the van, a man and a woman turned up to take me back into care. They explained that Dad hadn't been awarded custody of me and the authorities didn't think it was right that I should be living with him, especially as he was 'living in sin' with Olga. Dad said: 'You'll have to go with them. Don't worry, I'll sort it out.' But I'd only just got away from the kind of home they had in mind for me and I wasn't going back. I was only eight, and small for my age, but you'd be amazed at the strength I found that day. I screamed and kicked and clung on to anything I could find. Each time they prised my fingers free, I'd grab something else. Dad stood back for a while but in the end, he'd had enough and told them to leave me alone or else he'd have a go. So off they went and left me.

Of course they came back. They told me if I didn't go with them, they would put my dad in prison, and, having lived in the shadow of Brixton for a while, I didn't want that. They took me to Ella's. She didn't really want me, she just didn't want Dad to have me, and very soon she sent me back to the James's. I was gutted at the prospect of spending any more time with them and was preparing to run away when Dad arrived once more. He and Olga had got a special licence and were married, so I was allowed to return to them and a life with the circus.

TWO

Send in the Giraffe

Circuses and shows were to be my life for the next five years and like all circus kids I was expected to work for my keep. I became part of Dad's act. He would squeeze me into a tiny pedal car with him and drive us round the ring. He was dressed in a huge fur coat and when he jumped out he would snap open one of those theatrical top hats, which had been lying flat in the car. After bowing extravagantly to the crowd, he'd help me out and there was always a loud 'aah' from the audience as they realised I was dressed as a miniature version of him. To increase the illusion that we had packed an impossible amount into such a small car, I had to drag out a huge suitcase, which was again collapsible, opening it out as I emerged. The audience loved it and I relished the applause.

For 20 minutes or so between shows, while the punters were wandering around, I'd be in the sideshows, usually as the Giraffe-necked Woman. 'She' consisted of my mum's legs sticking out below a skirt, and some way above them, my head wearing make-up and a wig, on top of a long 'neck' made of a tin tube covered in African-style wooden necklaces. Sometimes I'd be Iffany the Spider Woman, which was my face, again made up like a woman, representing the head of a spider in the middle of its web. Of course we didn't want the punters to think there was anything dodgy going on, so I'd change my wig for a blonde one. I was always amazed at how easily people were taken in and some of the comments they made to each other were quite funny. But mostly my memory is of how boring it was just sitting there posing, and it was then that I learned to cat nap, something that has stood me in good stead ever since, especially on long flights.

Occasionally I would be loaned out to Uncle Tom, who had his own show, and there I'd be in charge of the mechanical organ with which he had to provide the characteristic fairground sound. I had to feed the sheets from the perforated cardboard music books into the mechanism and make sure it fed on to the pins that produced the sound. While that tune played through, I'd 'sling the G'. I never understood why it was called that but I was pretty good at it. I'd go out into the crowd while Uncle Tom did his spiel and if the customers were slow to come forward, I'd noisily persuade my 'mum', my Aunt Ethel, to take me to the show. We would pretend to pay in and that invariably prompted others to follow suit. Then it was another sheet of music, a change of clothes and back outside with Ethel to keep the crowds moving. While the show was on, I'd go round checking the canvas and making sure no one was doing a 'perimeter job' – creeping under the tent without paying.

Life with the circus may look glamorous from the outside, but mostly it was just hard work, long hours and plenty of discomfort with very little concession made to the fact you were just a kid. At times it seemed to be an endless procession of erecting the big top, tearing it down again, loading the trucks and heading off to the next site.

Dad and I travelled in the Morris Commercial, which had the engine and petrol tank inside. It only held about three gallons of fuel so we carried green cans filled with petrol in the cab. Dad could never be bothered to stop and fill up. He'd say: 'Check the petrol, Mike,' and I'd take the lid off and put a stick in to see how much was left. If it needed filling, I'd shove a funnel in and pour in the petrol while we drove along. The roads were pretty dodgy back then but luckily I didn't realise what would have happened if I'd spilled petrol onto the hot engine. If I had, I might have been much shakier.

For a while we toured the theatres in a show called *Front Page Personalities* with Dickie Henderson, the singer Hutch, a pair of newcomers called Morecambe and Wise and a young impressionist, Peter Sellers. He was my favourite because he used to imitate the characters in the radio show *Dick Barton – Special Agent*. At the end of the season, they all signed up for the next year but the management didn't renew the contracts of Morecambe and Wise, replacing them with Dave King, a popular comedian and singer who later did some acting and even popped up in *Coronation Street*. Back then he was the act that used to go in front of the curtain while Dad's knife-throwing set was erected behind it.

Eric Morecambe was fascinated by Dad's knives and called him 'Hatchet Baby'. They spent quite a lot of time together between shows, talking, laughing and playing poker. Dad also thought Eric showed a bit too much interest in Olga and one night, when he thought she was going out for a rendezvous with him, Dad hid all her shoes so she had to stay in. Years later, Eric and Ernie, by now the biggest names on TV, came to Leeds to sign copies of a book they were promoting. Dad pushed his way to the front of this long queue of people waiting patiently to get their books autographed and said: 'Hi, Eric, how you doing?' For a moment Eric thought it was just another punter but then his face lit up with that familiar grin, he did a double take and said: 'Hatchet Baby!' Even though Dad was about 80 by then and they hadn't met for at least 40 years, Eric remembered him straight away. Dad always did make an impact.

Also on the *Front Page Personalities* bill was a brilliant escapologist, Alan Allen, and a guy called Tommy 'Toes' Jacobson. Just like John Chambers in my grandfather's novelty show, Tommy had no arms. His speciality was to bring a bloke out of the audience, sit him on a chair, put a towel round him, then lather him up and shave him with a cut-throat razor – all with his feet. The climax of his act was to carefully place an apple on the head of a stooge then, as the lights went down and the drums rolled, bounce around on one leg clutching a .22 rifle with his other foot. It looked as though he had no control of the weapon at all and the audience were almost wetting themselves with nervous laughter as he hopped about, then they burst into loud, relief-filled applause as Tommy successfully shot the apple.

But to my young mind the most exciting part of the show was the Motorcycle Makowskis, a wall of death act who really captured my imagination and landed me in plenty of trouble.

Monday morning was set aside for rehearsals. Dad would always be first into the theatre because he didn't like people to see him working out his marks. He even wanted his fellow pros to think it was all off the cuff. In fact, he took tremendous care to make sure he had enough

room and a suitable angle to throw his chivs and hatchets. Some of the
stages were a bit small and it could take some time for him to find just
the right places for Olga and him to stand. While he was doing that,
Olga would take me to the local school and book me in.

If you can remember how daunting starting school is, you'll
understand what it was like being the new boy every single week. I
longed for the trips to Wales where there was no point in me going to
school because they spoke Welsh. But most weeks it would be the
same old routine. I'd get stuck in a class with a load of curious kids,
who at first just wanted to know what it was like living in the circus.
Then one of the boys, usually a big one, would get fed up because I
was getting too much attention on his patch, and a fight would start. I
was game but tiny, and I soon got fed up with the constant stream of
punch-ups and started to play hooky. It meant my formal education
was never up to much and I have to thank Olga for most of what I
learned. She taught me to read and write and I used to love filling
books with carefully crafted script.

Anyway, who needed school? I already knew what I wanted to be
– a wall of death rider – and you didn't need to go to school for that.
I soon became artful enough to keep out of Olga's way until she got
fed up with looking for me, then I'd hang around with the
Makowskis. Ken, who owned the act, used to let me help clean the
bikes. They were heavy old clutch-started Levises, painted red and
silver. I eventually got good at starting them up and I would hold
them revving in the wings so Ken could take them off me and roar
away.

The stagehands would haul the wall of death up into the 'gods' at an
angle to the stage so that everyone could look down as the bikes went
round inside. There was no safety net, so if a bike stalled the rider
dropped like a stone. In those days there were no health and safety
inspectors coming round to tell you what you could and couldn't do.
I remember a Spanish tightrope walker used to rig a wire from the
stage to the balcony, and the climax of her act was to walk out over the
audience and then slide backwards to the stage. If she'd fallen, she
would have landed in the laps of the paying customers, but that was
the thrill of it; the crowd's hearts would be in their mouths when
trapeze artists flew high above them without a net. We take too much

of the danger out of life these days and everything ends up as bland as fish and chips without salt and vinegar.

I badgered Ken for some time and eventually he agreed to take me up on the pillion during a rehearsal. It was breathtaking, scary and exhilarating at the same time. Only the speed of the bike kept us clinging to the wall as we raced round and round. When I got off my head was spinning and Ken said: 'Clear off and stay out of the way in case your dad comes.' The rides continued for about three months and I soon got used to the giddy feeling. I was wondering how long it would be before I could persuade Ken to let me have a go on my own, but my days as a motorbike star were soon to come to a jolting halt. One day as Ken and I were spiralling back down towards the stage, I heard a piercing scream that echoed round the empty theatre for ages. Olga had come looking for me and was horrified when she saw me hurtling around above her head. I got off with a big grin on my face but as soon as Dad turned up and realised what was going on, he yelled: 'You grinning ape. I'll soon wipe that off your face.' He did. After that I was a regular at school for a while.

Dad was not an easy man to please. He imposed arbitrary rules and if you broke them the punishment was swift and final, no leniency, no arguments. I remember I once had a Larry Adler harmonica. This was no tin-pot mouth organ, it was the real thing with stops on the end, and it was my pride and joy. I spent hours wandering around sucking and blowing into it until I started to get a few recognisable tunes. At the time my best mate was another circus kid, Jamoon, whose dad was a member of an Indian tumbling group from Doncaster. He shared my enthusiasm for the harmonica and we took it in turns to play, each impressed with the other's growing mastery. But when Dad found out I was letting Jamoon play, he immediately forbade me to lend it to him, adding: 'If you do, I'll give it to him.' I didn't understand what was so wrong and Jamoon and I carried on playing tunes together, keeping a wary eye open for the old man. But inevitably he caught us one day. Spotting the danger, I grabbed the harmonica and tried to make out it had been taken against my will, but Dad took it off me and threw it to my mate. I hated Jamoon from then on, especially as the little sod wouldn't let me have a go on *his* harmonica.

Dad planned for me to be a knife-thrower. He had a set of chivs made for me and even though I wasn't particularly interested, I used to practise just to please him. He never gave me any advice or offered a word of encouragement. In fact his presence seemed to make me worse – you could guarantee that if he was around the knives, which had been sticking in before, would start to bounce off the board. He'd watch for a few minutes then wander off muttering things like: 'That boy will never make anything of himself.' I knew I'd upset him and was angry with myself for being so useless. Then I'd practise even harder until I got it right. One day I spotted Olga walking down towards the paper shop at the end of the yard near our winter quarters in Brixton. I followed her and stood over the road, and as she came out, I let the chivs go. I'll never forget her face as they whacked into the wooden door surround. After the initial shock she flew into a rage, screaming at me. I couldn't understand what the fuss was about. I thought she'd be pleased – I'd got the bloody things to stick in, and from 20 to 30 ft away. You just can't please some people.

My heart was never in knife-throwing. If I couldn't be a wall of death rider, I wanted to fly on the high trapeze and I became quite skilled at it. Reluctantly Dad built me a rig in the yard at Brixton and whenever we were there I would work on it. I guess I hoped he would see that I was quite good and let me develop an act. He didn't seem to notice so one day, when he and Olga had gone up to the West End to do some shopping, I started to work up a routine that I would show them when they got back. I worked all day until my ankles and toes were chafed and sore. As soon as I heard them return, I climbed up on the trailer and waited, glancing out of the corner of my eye until they were looking my way. When I was sure they had noticed me, I swung out, flinging myself forward, spreading my legs and catching myself by my feet. If I'd missed, I'd have gone headfirst into the prison wall! I did the full routine, swinging by my toes and heels, eight feet off the ground with only an old mattress below me, finishing with a perfect dismount. Olga came out and said: 'You've been working hard', but Dad didn't say a word. Years later Olga told me she had asked him to raise the trapeze so I could keep practising. Instead, he went out the next day and took the rig down. I never did find out why.

It was probably about then that I ran away for a couple of days. Monty and I had never got on but when Ella dumped me back with the James's just before Dad married Olga, I think he realised how unhappy I was. He used to come to the bedroom to cheer me up when Matey got on my case and perhaps if I hadn't gone off to join Dad again, we might have become closer. Anyway, I decided it would be nice to see how he was and hitchhiked to Warlingham. Monty was surprised to see me but seemed pleased and when I told him I'd run away from Dad, he tried to persuade me to move back in with him. That was the last thing I wanted and I said I was going back to Brixton. He gave me all the money he had, three shillings and sixpence, for something to eat and my fare. When I turned up at the caravan, nothing was said. It was as though I'd never been away. Apparently Olga had been worried but Dad wouldn't let her phone anyone, saying: 'Leave him. He'll be back.'

Although it had its ups and downs, life with the shows was my element and, like all kids, I thought it would go on forever. But it was too good to last. Eventually the authorities stuck their official noses in, decided I wasn't getting enough education and sent me to stay with Dad's brother, Uncle George and his wife Aunty Brenda in Clapham. When Dad had a circus, they were the advance agents, going ahead of the show to find the 'tober', a piece of vacant land near a centre of population that looked suitable to pitch a big top. Then they would post bills everywhere they could, and some places they shouldn't, so by the time we hit town there was already an air of anticipation. They also had a furniture and antique shop in Clapham Park Road, and when that was pulled down, they moved to Streatham Vale. Aunty Brenda still has the antique shop there, Norman's Corner.

When they first moved in, Uncle George looked out of the front window above the shop and saw a sign over the road pointing to Streatham Crematorium. He didn't fancy being reminded of his mortality each time he looked out of his window, so that night he went out with his tools, took the sign down and threw it on to the railway embankment. The council put up a new sign the next week but when he took that one down, they didn't bother any more. George died a year before my dad, and sure enough, he didn't need a sign to end up in the right place.

They had two children, Pat and Russell. Cousin Russell was a year older than me and excelled at sport. He was a good boxer, held records for swimming, and he played football for England schoolboys, youth, Under-21 and Under-23, and was on the books at Tottenham Hotspur as an amateur. He even had a letter from Spurs' double-winning manager Bill Nicholson, who wanted him to turn pro. His mum wouldn't let him become a footballer because there wasn't enough money in it in those days. I guess she was right because he went on to be an accountant and now Russell has retired, a wealthy man with a string of big cars, a Harley Davidson motorbike and a luxury flat. But playing for Spurs . . .

He was also good academically and, when I followed him at Hazelrigg School, Mr Mills, the headmaster, was rubbing his hands at the thought of another member of the family coming in to boost the school's performance. I soon brought him back to the real world.

I took my eleven-plus exam for the grammar school when I was briefly back with Dad and attending Kennington Tech. I failed, which wasn't a big surprise. I was never any good at exams. I had no interest in them. Who needed them? I was going to be a circus performer or, by this time, maybe a sportsman. School was irrelevant. I was already working all day Saturday at Moore's furniture sales on Streatham Hill.

When Dad and Olga went off to the States aboard the luxury liner *Canberra* on another contract, they farmed me out again, this time to Olga's elder sister Barbara and her husband Harry, who lived on a caravan site on the outskirts of Datchet, near Windsor. I didn't realise then, but that marked the end of my life in the circus. At the time, things just seemed to be following a familiar pattern – live with Dad for a while, then be sent off to stay with someone else while he made some cash.

I got on well with my new family although we had a bit of a stormy introduction. Within days of my arrival I'd started school in Wraysbury. I was nearly 13 years old and the only boy in the school still in short trousers. It was bad enough being the new kid again, without giving the others such an obvious target for teasing. I went home and said I wasn't going to school until they bought me some long trousers. I got a good hiding but I refused to budge, so in the end Aunty Barbara relented and took me to Slough to buy my first pair of men's trousers.

There was another initial hiccup at school. We were in a reading class and the lad next to me had picked out an annual based on the popular comic, *The Eagle*. It seemed much more interesting than the book I'd chosen and as I looked over his shoulder, he turned to a picture of my dad throwing knives round the TV personality Macdonald Hastings. Without thinking, I said: 'That's my dad.' My classmate looked at me scornfully. He clearly thought I was trying to be flash and immediately involved the other kids in taking the piss out of me. He pointed to a picture of Buckingham Palace and said: 'I suppose that's your house?' The kerfuffle brought the teacher over and no matter how much I insisted, 'But it *is* my dad,' even she wouldn't believe me. Later I backed up my story by taking the kid in the next seat into the playground for a punch-up but it was only after the teacher had checked with Aunty Barbara that they realised I wasn't the lying little toe-rag they'd thought. Just a little toe-rag.

Once that was sorted out, the other kids seemed to accept me and the next year was to prove the most enjoyable I had at school. I was involved in plenty of sport and was quite successful at it. I represented the county at gymnastics and athletics. I managed to get in the football team in the age category above me, and again represented the county. I also got involved in boxing and won the county championship. I'd first watched boxing in the old fairground booths. I used to love seeing the guys, all ego and cockiness, get a battering from the broken-nosed veterans who hardly broke sweat. I'd wanted to have a go myself but this was the first time I'd pulled on the gloves to take someone on. At that age, boxing is mainly about fear and having been involved in countless brawls at school and with my brother, I was no longer worried about getting hurt.

It was good for my street cred that I could box, especially as I'd also taken up dancing. If the other kids hadn't known I was quite handy, it might have meant a few more fights to defend myself against the accusations of being a 'poofter'. Not that we had any idea what a poofter was, or anything else to do with sex. We heard that a 13-year-old girl at school had got pregnant but none of my group knew what that meant. All we knew was that it was trouble and to be avoided. To me, girls were just good for dancing partners. I'd joined the Bob and Ada Unsworth junior formation team, who had classes at Slough Community Centre. Their team was the best in Britain at the time, and I took to it immediately.

Soon it was time for me to take my thirteen-plus exam, a last opportunity to get into the grammar school. But I had no chance. Not that it bothered me. I just kept grinning my way through. One teacher said: 'Norman, you need this exam or you will end up as a labourer.' I replied: 'No, I just need my arms and legs, because I'm going to be a sportsman.'

Life was good. I was a somebody, skipping religious instruction, music, metalwork and woodwork for sports training, and certain I was headed for a career as a footballer. It all came to a grinding halt when Dad sent word that Olga's mother needed help running her boarding house in Leeds and I was the one chosen to provide it.

THREE

Black-haired Susie and the Brunette

9 Woodhouse Square in Leeds, was a large, three-storey Victorian house that was by far the biggest place I'd ever lived in. Olga's dad, who'd been born in Switzerland, had recently died. I gather there had been quite a lot of money in the family at one time and, according to family legend, they'd owned a big hotel, which had one bedroom for every day of the year. Woodhouse Square was something of a comedown from that. It was a guesthouse catering mainly for navvies and labourers. Although she was in her 70s, Olga's mum still did most of the work. She was only 5 ft tall, with bushy, grey hair and glasses hanging round her neck on a chain, but she was still strong enough to lift the huge pot of stew she kept simmering on the old black Yorkist cooking range. The guests all called her 'Ma' and treated her politely, never swearing in her presence. She was kind to me and I soon started to call her Ma as well. Before long I'd settled into my new life and was feeling at home.

I went to school at Blackman Lane and the other kids were OK with me, despite my Cockney accent. I soon had a couple of good mates. Brian Holmes came from a well-known rugby league family. His brother John was one of the all-time greats with Leeds and Great Britain, and another brother, Philip, played for Leeds, Blackpool and Batley. Brian also went on to play professionally. In contrast my other pal, Dave Flanagan, had a problem with low calcium and was always breaking bones. At one time he had two broken arms and a broken bone in his neck, yet incredibly his main ambition was to go into the services – and the RAF accepted him! He and Brian still keep in touch.

I'm not as diligent as they are – I enjoy meeting up with old friends, but tend to shy away from regular contact.

My disappointment at leaving Wraysbury soon passed. I was playing football at school, although there was no opportunity to box there, something I wanted to start again. I wasn't sure how to go about it until one Saturday afternoon, when I was watching the amateur bouts they used to show on BBC TV and heard one of the commentators say that Geoff Towers, a cracking little England international flyweight, was from the Market and District Boys' Club in Leeds. I got the address from the phone book and went along. That was the real start of boxing for me. I had 66 fights as an amateur and only lost 17. I was a decent enough fighter and reached a few semi-finals. Although I never quite made it to a championship, I was good enough to know that this was what I wanted to do. Football began to take a back seat. I'd been accepted to train at Elland Road under manager Bill Lambton but he insisted that I'd have to give up boxing if I wanted to go on and play for Leeds United. That finished me. As soon as someone tells me I can't do something, it makes me even more determined. Anyway I probably liked a scrap too much to have made it as a footballer. Any notions that I'd have become a Leeds United superstar if I'd made a different decision were dismissed some years later when I played in a charity match with their ex-players association. I thought I'd done quite well but in the dressing-room afterwards, Eddie Gray said: 'Mickey, don't give up the day job.'

Brian Holmes and I had a bet to see who would represent the county first and I nicked it by a week. I won the Yorkshire title and got my colours just before he was picked for the rugby team. I went on to make the national semi-finals of the Boys' Clubs championship, where I lost to the eventual winner. The amateur game was far less regulated then than it is now and there certainly weren't as many cups and medals handed out, unlike today when kids seem to pick up a prize just for turning up. To win a major championship you had to win three bouts in a day. Only then did you get a trophy. If you were beaten in any of the earlier contests you didn't even get a bit of paper to show for your efforts.

Even at the ABA championships, the pinnacle for amateur boxers, you had to fight the semi-final and final on the same day. The ABAs were a big deal when I was a youngster, one of the days in the sporting calendar that people looked forward to. They were always held at Wembley Arena, which would be packed, and the finals were shown live on TV. It's a sad reflection on amateur boxing that the finals are now staged in places like the Barnsley Metrodome and are largely ignored by television. I think it's time the amateur game changed its attitude and followed the example set in some countries, where they include amateur bouts on professional bills. I've seen this in action and it works well for the fighters, promoters and fans. The amateurs have always been paranoid that pro managers would steal their best boxers, but that happens anyway, and a joint promotion is the only way I can see amateurs getting the necessary exposure and cash to survive and recruit new fighters. Attitudes must change. I recall when I first started refereeing I used to go to the Meanwood Boys' Club in Leeds. It helped me get experience and it was also good for the boxers to work with a real referee. But it was blocked because the authorities warned the club they would no longer be affiliated if they used someone from the professional ranks. I thought that was crazy, the kind of thinking that's put amateur boxing almost out of existence.

It was about this stage of my life that I made my first fumbling attempts at sex. Ma loved to play cards. She was like a character in an old black-and-white movie – a tiny old lady in a smoke-filled room, taking money off huge navvies by out-bluffing them at poker. She and I would often play on a Sunday afternoon with Carol, the girl who used to look after my dad's dogs, which were kept in the cellar. Carol and I usually took no notice of each other, but one afternoon, for some reason I stretched out my legs under the table and trapped her ankle. There was suddenly electricity between us. I gave her a nod, she nodded back and, at the end of that hand, we made our excuses and left Ma playing patience.

As soon as we reached the cellar Carol and I started to grope each other, admittedly rather amateurishly. I was just slowing down enough to get things sorted out for a knee-trembler against the wall when Brian Holmes's voice came from the top of the cellar stairs: 'Mickey, what are you doing?' That wrecked the mood, I can tell you! Carol and I never got it together again and sadly she committed suicide some time later. I hope it was nothing to do with my two left hands.

About a year later, Dad and Olga came up to help Ma out full time. I didn't realise she was getting too frail to cope, even with me doing more and more of the errands. I thought she would go on forever but I guess it was getting too much for her. It wasn't long before Dad and I were at loggerheads. I'd got used to doing what I pleased once I'd finished my bits and pieces for Ma but Dad wanted to be in control. I remember getting so angry one time that I clenched my fists, half ready to throw a punch at him. He spotted what I'd done and got that icy look in his eye. 'Fancy your chances, do you?' he snapped. 'Even if you did manage to beat me with your fists, I'd just go downstairs, get a lump hammer and break your back.' I unclenched my hands, apologised and slunk out. I was still angry but I was scared of Dad. I knew the fact that I was his son wouldn't make any difference if it came to a showdown.

Each day when I arrived back from school, I would call out, 'Hiya, Ma. I'm home.' One day there was no reply. Instead Dad appeared from the cellar. 'Where's Ma, Dad?' I asked. 'She's dead,' he said and walked past me. Just like that. No letting me down gently. I didn't even get the chance to say goodbye – the undertaker had already removed her body. I was shattered. Ma had looked after me. She'd been kind to me, especially recently when she realised the problems I'd been having with Dad. She'd renewed my confidence every time he'd said I wouldn't make anything of myself. I was determined he wouldn't see that I was upset so I went outside and cried. The funeral was at Lawnswood crematorium and I used to go up there and sit by her plaque, shedding a tear because she was no longer there to guide me as I tried to work out what to do with my life.

Dad and Olga took over the house. They kicked out the boarders, even though some of them had been staying there for eight years, and turned it into flats. I decided I'd had enough and made up my mind to leave. I got down my battered suitcase, covered with Cunard stickers that Dad had given me, and packed. Once more everything I owned was contained in one case.

I tried to slip out quietly but as I got to the first landing I heard Dad behind me.

'Mike!' he barked. 'Where d'ya think you're going?'

I was terrified but this time there could be no stepping down. I managed to say: 'I'm leaving, Dad.'

'If you walk out that door, you don't come back.'

'I know.' I turned and walked slowly down the stairs and out the door. I was 14.

I can't remember ever being more frightened. That night I just went across the square and slept rough. Then I bedded down on a bench in the local park for a couple of nights. I had enough about me to get a wash in the morning and a couple of neighbours gave me a cup of tea and a bite to eat. But I needed somewhere to stay, and that meant getting a job so I could pay for it. The next couple of years taught me a lot about looking after myself, and forced me to become an expert at surviving by one means or another.

My first job was as a van boy at Martins' laundry, which paid me four pounds ten shillings a week. That allowed me to rent a bedsit off a German woman. It was near the police station in Bellevue Road and cost me 30 bob a week. I earned an extra pound a week doing a paper round – you got ten bob for six days and an extra ten bob for Sundays because no one wanted to do them. I topped up my money by taking any boxing prizes I won to Walt Barrow, the landlord of the Plasterer's Arms in Skinner Lane. He ran a raffle on Friday night and would give me two or three quid from that.

Things were still so tight that I couldn't afford to put the fire on in the bedsit. On cold days I'd get wrapped up in bed to keep warm. One Saturday morning I was idling away my time in the centre of Leeds, watching the traffic go by, when I noticed that the copper on point duty had left his cape hanging on a railing. It looked wonderfully warm, so the next time he turned his back I rolled it up, stuck it inside my jacket and legged it. I knew I couldn't wear it outside, so I took the numbers off the collar and used it as an extra blanket on my bed. The problem was that Bob Farquarson, one of the bobbies who had a flat downstairs, had taken to popping in to keep an eye on me. He soon spotted the cape. I stammered: 'It's not yours, Bob. I was cold. You can take it back,' and started to roll it up. He looked at me sternly. 'How the hell can I, Mickey? You've taken the numbers off so I don't know who it belongs to. You'd better keep it, but don't ever take it out of this room.'

Apart from Bob's reassuring interest, the thing that made the bedsit bearable was its location next door to a nurses' hostel. Some of the girls took a shine to me and would take me upstairs to introduce me to what life is all about. When I think how much women came to mean to me – and the bother they got me into – it's strange that up to then I was really naïve. I enjoyed my 'education' with the nurses but to be honest, I still wasn't that bothered about getting a girlfriend. I didn't have time – I was too wrapped up in my sport and making a living. But gradually women started to become a major part of my life, starting with Nina.

By this time I'd moved in with an Asian family on Brudenell Grove. My German landlady had put my rent up and though a rent tribunal took pity on me, my victory didn't last long because she made my life such a misery I had to move out. I'd also changed jobs. At the back of my mind I remembered that Ma had insisted I should get an apprenticeship. She was about the only person who had taken any interest in my future. She hadn't even laughed when I said I wanted to be a professional sportsman, suggesting the best way into that would be to join the forces. I thought it was quite a good idea but Dad wouldn't let me go in as a boy entrant. He wanted me to be an officer trainee, which meant more exams, so it was out of the question. The next suggestion was the merchant navy – not great for sport, but I guess they wanted to get me out of their hair. Again Dad had delusions of adequacy and wanted me to go in as an artificer but that cost money and came to nothing. Dad had always said that if he hadn't been in show business he would have been a carpenter so when I started thinking about getting a trade, I decided I'd like to be a joiner. People advised me to go into engineering, saying it would include joinery, which was true at one stage but not by the time I signed up for a six-year apprenticeship with Sykes and Hepworth on Royal Park Road.

I started on 29 December, my birthday, and I wasn't thrilled with the way it changed my life. To start with, the work was a lot harder. I was working on the furnaces and the sweat poured off me. As a van boy, I would start work at nine o'clock but now I had to be in at half past seven and didn't finish until five, with only half an hour for dinner. I also worked half a day on Saturday and for all that I walked away with two pounds ten shillings. By the time I'd paid my rent I only had eleven shillings left for the rest of the week, so the ducking and diving had to go into overdrive.

I kept on delivering papers and Arthur, who was stepping up, handed on the 'gofer' round at work, which meant I had to fetch and carry for my workmates. It could be a nice little earner. Arthur marked my card on which shops would give you a discount or free food, and advised me that if I kept in with the other men, they might give me half a crown on Friday for running their errands. I was a cheerful little sod, so that wasn't too hard. To look at my skinny little body, you would have thought I was starving but in fact I was eating well. Some of the guys would bring in extra sandwiches for me, and on Wednesdays and Fridays I'd go to the chip shop where I would get ten per cent back in cash and free fish and chips for myself.

Opposite the factory was the Royal Park pub, run by the Dent sisters. They were a couple of strapping lasses who stood for no nonsense and were tough enough to survive without bouncers even though it was a rough old pub. Round the back there was a bowling green in a big garden and one day the girls were complaining because they didn't have time to keep it tidy. 'He's a good gardener, aren't you Mickey?' my mate Brian Wheatley said. I was a bit taken aback because I'd never done any gardening before, but I grinned, agreed and found myself with a weekend job. I rushed straight round to the library because I needed a book to find out how to tell the weeds from the flowers – I still do – but it turned out to be quite easy money. I would just mow the grass, pull out a few weeds, trim the hedge, water when necessary and generally keep the place respectable, for which I pocketed a pound a week that the taxman never knew about.

The lads at work took to me and showed a lot of interest in my boxing. I went to the Boulevard in Hull for the Fish Fryers' show, which was a big annual event. I gave a local lad a right hammering and was presented with a gold-coloured clock in the shape of a penny-farthing bike. This would earn me a few bob at the Plasterer's Arms, but it was the fanciest prize I'd ever won and I wanted to show it off to my mates before cashing it in. When I took it into the tool room, the lads were clearly impressed. One of them said: 'You did OK then, Mickey?' Full of myself I replied: 'I fucking arseholed him.' At that, a voice that sounded like a cross between a school matron and a vicar sounded behind me: 'I beg your pardon!' I'd not noticed that Peggy, a woman who made all the lads watch their Ps and Qs, was working on the surface grinder. The lads all roared with laughter, especially as the cocky fighter immediately flushed bright red and looked very meek, wishing the floor would open and swallow him up.

I first noticed Nina as I walked to work. She lived on Royal Park Road and had long brunette hair tied up in a ponytail, and a great figure considering she was only 14 years old. All the young lads wanted to take her out but since I was working I had the edge, and pretty soon we were dating. As I said, I didn't know much about girls and even less about things like the age of consent, and it wasn't long before we were lovers. I gave her a key to my place and on Sunday mornings she'd tell her mum she was going to church but instead come round to my place and slip into my bed before I was really awake. As the song says, 'beats a cup of coffee for starting off the day'.

Her mum, Winnie, was broad-minded and when she realised we were an item, she said I could do up their loft and live there rent-free. She obviously knew what was going on because one day she called me over and gave me a Littlewoods pools envelope. 'I don't do the pools,' I said. She laughed and said: 'Take it, Mickey. And be careful.' When I got up to my room and opened the envelope I saw it contained contraceptives. Winnie also realised I was unhappy at work. She was a director at a transmission engineers, Peter Rayners, and said that if I could get out of my apprenticeship, she could get me a place as a tool room apprentice, which was a better job with more money. The governors at Sykes and Hepworth were a pain and wanted to keep me to my six-year agreement but the works manager, Frank Eddison, was a great bloke and when I explained the situation to him, he persuaded them to let me go.

My new job was great. I was in the tool room with Jim Rennison and Don Lofts, and my lathe was by a sash window so I could nip out to the shops to get Mars Bars for the other lads. I'm often struck by how my life seems to have little coincidences in it, with people popping up in all sorts of uncanny circumstances. For instance, Jim Rennison had a son, also Jim, who is a great friend of Keith, who became my brother-in-law. Jim works for Anchor car hire, and it was one of their managers who nicked Karen, the girl I went out with for eight and a half years. Then there was Brian who, along with Big John, was one of my best mates at Rayners. I lost touch with both of them, but years later when

I was training a kids' football team, one of the players said 'My granddad knows you,' and it turned out to be Brian.

Next door to Rayners was Tainton's factory, where they used to make clothes for Grattans mail order catalogue, and one of the great things about being next to a window was that I could see all the girls go in and out. One girl in particular caught my eye. I thought she was stunning and christened her 'black-haired Susie' after a woman who was making the tabloid headlines for having an affair with an officer on the Cunard line. Before long, I started to time my trips to the shop to make sure I bumped into her. She told me her name was Rita. She was a machinist and used to model the clothes. I was very struck and soon I'd persuaded her to meet me in the boiler room, which became our regular lunchtime rendezvous. The lads used to chuckle as I skipped in and out the window, warning me: 'Be careful, Mickey. Remember you're living with one of the directors and courting her daughter!'

In fact, it had gone beyond courting. Nina and I were engaged. Winnie had taken us to Harrogate to buy a ring that set her back about a hundred and forty quid, a hell of a lot of money in those days. Pretty soon, Rita and I were also unofficially engaged – back then girls wouldn't let you get your leg over unless you promised to marry them. It took a bit of juggling to make it work. I would tell each of them I was training for a fight while I was with the other, and I also had to fit in some training. I was knackered but having too much fun to stop. However, things were about to get even more complicated.

I was selected to box against Wales at the Hightown barracks in Wrexham. Any boxer will tell you how important it is to tape your hands properly, but I didn't realise and used to split a hole in an old crepe bandage for my thumb, then wrap it round my fist, tying a knot with my spare hand and my teeth. I paid the price for my ignorance. That night I not only got beaten on points, I smashed my hand up. They offered to take me to hospital in Wrexham but I said I'd prefer to get it sorted out back in Leeds, so I found myself in the famous 'Jimmys' about to have surgery on my knuckle. I knew I had a much bigger problem than a sore fist. My two fiancées were bound to want to visit me. I couldn't risk that, so I rang Rita and told her I'd be upset if she saw me like that and would contact her as soon as I came out of hospital.

In those pre-waiting list times I had an artificial knuckle fitted in a couple of days, and the surgeon must have done a good job because it's still there today. Nina was very attentive. I wasn't in much pain and enjoyed her fussing round, at the same time quietly congratulating myself on how well I'd handled the situation. The day before I was discharged, I phoned Rita and arranged to meet her. I thought I'd cracked it but then the next bombshell broke. Nina had been studying at design college and one day she came bouncing in saying: 'Mickey, I've passed my exams and got a job.'

'Great,' I said. 'Where are you working?'

'At Tainton's, next door to you!'

FOUR

The Ups and Downs of a Journeyman

Anyone with half a brain would have realised I couldn't get away with having two fiancées working in the same firm, and next door to where I worked. But I've felt bulletproof most of my life and believed things would work out. After an initial panic I thought I had things sorted again. And to be fair, I was successful for a while. Four days to be exact.

I knew the designers and machinists didn't mix much, so they were unlikely to get talking to each other. They were also working different shifts – Rita from eight to four, Nina from nine to five thirty. I was off work while my knuckle healed, so I arranged to meet Rita at four, walk her home and have a quick kiss and a cuddle before shooting back down to meet Nina and go home with her on the bus.

That was fine until the Friday, when they both finished at four. I invented an excuse and told Rita I wouldn't be able to meet her after work but said I'd have a drink with her in the Smyths Arms at dinnertime. Nina didn't drink, so I reckoned I would be safe. I slipped in the side door of the pub so there was no chance of Nina seeing me and took a seat in the snug where I could see the door. Some of the girls I knew from Tainton's came in. Something was up. They walked straight past me without a word and huddled by the bar in a sudden babble of conversation and laughter. I was still trying to figure out what was going on when the door slammed open, almost tearing off its hinges. It was Nina. She wasn't happy.

'You bastard!' she screamed, struggling to pull her engagement ring off her finger. 'You bloody bastard!' The ring came flying in my general direction and she turned and stormed out. I was gobsmacked but had enough about me to scramble around and find the ring before going after her. If the worse came to worst, I figured the ring would be worth a bob or two at the pawnbrokers.

I learned later that both girls had been in the canteen at the same time that morning. Nina was telling one of her pals about my operation and her friend said that, by coincidence, Rita also had a boyfriend who boxed and had hurt his hand. It hadn't taken long for them to put two and two together and on the count of four the pair of them were scrapping in the middle of the floor until Lily, the manageress at Tainton's, stepped in and parted them.

I caught up with Nina and managed to tell her there had been a big mistake. She gradually calmed down and I gave her back the ring, promising to meet her after work. I then slipped in the window at Rayners to find out what was being said. The lads were killing themselves laughing and one of them said: 'Mickey, there's been murder on here. Lily's been round looking for you and she said she's going to cut your balls off when she catches up with you. And wait till Winnie finds out what's been going on!'

At four o'clock I waited across the road from the factory and Nina marched over, took my arm and led me off to the bus stop. She obviously wanted to show the rest of the girls that she'd won, but I'd made up my mind I preferred Rita and told Nina on the bus that it wasn't going to work. She burst into tears and I sat there shuffling under the gaze of the other passengers until we reached her stop. She ran off and I dashed back to try and make things up with Rita. If I wasn't careful, I was going to go from two fiancées to none in the space of a few hours.

This was going to be tricky. I'd never been in Rita's house. I knew her old man, Bill, didn't like her going out with boys, especially boys like me. In fact it was 18 months before he let me across the threshold. I used to wait on the corner of the street and her little brother, Keith – all ears and cowboy hat – acted as messenger between us. I'd slip him a few bob every now and again to keep his mouth shut and he was great, never letting on once. Her mum, Joyce, was also brilliant. She would make sandwiches for Rita to give me after I walked her home, and I'd have them for supper back at my digs. It's no wonder I still see Joyce regularly, and Keith is like a brother to me.

As I approached the house to make my peace I knew I would have to knock on the door. The closer I got the more my bottle started to go. Had she told her dad what had happened? Would he open the door? What would he do to me? My trot slowed to a walk and that gradually decreased in pace as the possible scenarios – all of them violent, with me as the victim – flashed through my mind. I bullied myself into knocking on the door. A bloke built like a brick outhouse answered. He was Joe Desborough, a family friend, who was even scarier than Rita's dad. By this time I was shaking and ready to run. I heard a strange voice somewhere inside my head ask if Rita was in, while my half-numb brain urged me to concentrate, to look for the first sign that would signal the need to bolt. Strangely Joe didn't seem to notice my complete funk. He just went in and got Rita. She was a bit red-eyed but was probably as afraid of her dad realising I was there as I was, because she mouthed to her mum that she wouldn't be long and came outside. She wasn't pleased to see me and for about ten minutes I had to stand there and take it while this very feminine, attractive young girl went at me in language that would have made a navvy look up. Between the expletives, the message seemed to be that if I thought she was ever going out with me again, I must be dafter than I looked.

I let her have her say before explaining that I'd dumped Nina and Rita was the one I really loved. It took some doing, but slowly she came round and agreed to meet me the following day. I have to admit, I felt pretty good when I said cheerio to her and started back towards town. Then it dawned on me that I didn't have anywhere to sleep that night. I wondered if I might be able to make it up with Nina until I found somewhere new to live, but when I reached her house my suitcases were already packed and on the doorstep.

A mate helped me to find some digs and from then on Rita kept a close eye on me to make sure there were no more shenanigans. We made the engagement official and started saving to get married. I knew I had to keep my nose clean. That wasn't too hard – the episode with Nina had reduced my appetite for more than one girlfriend at a time, at least for a while. It was much harder to take Rita's constant complaints about my boxing. She hated all sport but thought boxing was particularly barbaric, especially when I came home cut and bruised. In one ABA championship fight I was up against a lad called

Len Mason. We had a right war. I knocked him down a couple of times and he put me down three times. My gum shield was fairly primitive then – just a bit of rubber that smelled and tasted horrible – and he ripped my mouth open. I had five stitches on the outside of my mouth and three inside. When Rita saw me she blew her top and said I had to give up fighting. I resisted but she went on so long that I finally gave in, and after a few more fights never boxed as an amateur again.

As with most young couples, our life together was overshadowed by a chronic lack of cash. In those days, if you got married on the first Saturday in April the government refunded all your previous year's tax. I'd been working out how important that would be for us and it must have been on my mind when Rita and I went out for a walk one evening. We were just chatting vaguely about getting married when I suddenly realised there were only about three and a half weeks to the deadline, and being a hopeless romantic reminded her that if we didn't put the banns up that week, we would have to wait another year. We went straight home and started to make plans. The arrangements were made in a hell of a rush. It must have been very tough on Rita's mum. The family weren't well off and to find the money for a wedding just like that can't have been easy, especially as Joyce did it without telling Bill that she paid for it.

The wedding was on 2 April at St Bartholomew's Church on Wesley Road in Leeds. It was snowing. We were due to get married at three o'clock and at twenty past, I was ready to go home because Rita hadn't turned up. I was fuming. It crossed my mind that she'd stood me up at the altar as an elaborate revenge for all I'd put her through with Nina. Her mum arrived just as I was about to call it a day and explained that the taxi had broken down. I didn't say anything because I could see that Joyce was feeling anything but the radiant mother of the bride – she was hot and flustered and there was a big damp patch on her smart new suit where she'd slipped over and landed on her backside in the snow. It was like something from one of those Jeremy Beadle shows on TV. I had made the classic mistake of leaving a big sale price sticker on the sole of my new shoes, which should have been enough to make even Rita's dad laugh. You never saw Bill smile. He's serious in all the wedding photographs except one – he allowed himself a little smirk when he was certain that I'd taken Rita off his hands.

All our savings and the tax rebate went on buying a house. It was a bungalow in Farsley, just outside Leeds, which we bought for two thousand, five hundred pounds from our solicitor. That left us cleaned out so it was a bit of a blow when he sent me a bill for twenty-five pounds for his services. That might not seem a lot now, but I was only earning seven pounds a week and I had visions of the bailiffs being the first visitors to our new home.

I'd had no contact with Dad since walking out when I was 14. Olga had got in touch occasionally and gave me a gold lighter and cigarette case on my 21st birthday. But she'd annoyed me when I phoned to tell her that I was engaged to Rita. She replied: 'That's great, but I don't think she's for you. You could do a lot better for yourself, Michael.' I didn't invite them or any of my relatives to the wedding – my best man was Rita's uncle Len. I didn't think my family would want to come, although later Dad told me he wished he'd been given the chance. But I'd changed, and I was worried he might turn up at the wedding and say something to spoil the day. We might have started arguing and I didn't want that.

Still, now I needed a loan, urgently. I had to swallow my pride and approach him. I asked Olga if she thought Dad would help. 'It's up to him,' she said. 'You'll have to ask him.'

It was strange meeting him again. I think he was pleased to see me, but he didn't want to show it and was cool and matter of fact. He wouldn't say either way about the loan, leaving it to Olga. She agreed but put me under pressure again within three weeks by asking for the money back! To make things worse, Rita fell pregnant with our first son, Tony, a month after we got married.

I missed boxing, especially the craic with the other lads. I hankered to get back in the ring and much as she hated the idea, Rita really couldn't argue when I suggested that if I turned professional it would help us out of our financial difficulties. I went to see Trevor Callighan, a local promoter and manager, who has looked after champions Alan Richardson and Tom Collins, and is now chairman of the Central Area Council. Trevor's a nice guy and gently told me that he couldn't take on any more fighters. In other words he had enough problems without me. He suggested I should try Tommy Miller at the Farmyard Inn in Bradford. I was worried that my age might be the problem, so when I went to see Tommy, I knocked off a couple of years. Later, I realised I needn't have lied. Tommy didn't give a monkey's – if you had two legs, two arms and a pulse, he would sign you. Tommy's in his late 80s now, as fit as a butcher's dog and the oldest licence holder in the country. He agreed to give me my start as a journeyman pro: have gloves, will travel – anywhere.

The first stop was Hull for six threes against a lad from London called Ricky McCullough. I was paid twenty quid. By now I was working night shifts at Towlers in Rodley because they paid better and none of the directors were the mother of my jilted fiancée. I got in a shift and a couple of hours' sleep before Tommy picked me up at eleven to get me to the weigh-in for one o'clock. I came in at eight stone twelve, and Tommy said: 'I'll see you at the stadium at seven. Go to the pictures or something.' Instead I went to a local park and pulled a couple of benches together. I ate my sandwiches, drank a bottle of Mackeson and smoked a cigarette before settling down for a few more hours' kip. We athletes have to look after our bodies.

When I got back to the stadium, I found my bout was down as the final fight, after the top of the bill, when the punters are rushing to the bar before it closes. I wasn't worried about the indignity of my billing, but if I went on last I would miss my shift, so I persuaded promoter Sid Gould to put me on first. I beat Ricky on points but six three-minute rounds seemed like an eternity. I'd used up so much nervous energy in the dressing-room, and the fight lasted twice as long as I'd ever been before, so by the time the ref lifted my arm I was dead on my feet. I remember thinking as I clambered on the train back to Leeds: 'If that's six rounds, I'll never go fifteen.'

Training was difficult because of the night work, although I enjoyed putting on a tracksuit and going running at two in the morning when I had a break. Even the normally mucky city streets were fresh at that time of the day. I had one more fight while I was on nights, but I was completely knackered and decided I was making enough from boxing to allow me to take the cut in wages that came from switching to the day shift.

That second fight was against Danny Hackett at the National Sporting Club in London. It was my first defeat and reminded Rita how much she loathed boxing. The day before I was sparring with

Lloyd Walford, the number one light-heavyweight in the country. He caught me with a solid hook that smashed my nose. I used to bleed easily anyway, and it took some time before I could stop the flow, but I didn't want to miss out on the money and went ahead with the fight. Sure enough, Danny's first big punch landed square on my nose and there was no way to stop the bleeding, especially as his jab seemed to be drawn to the middle of my face like a laser-guided bomb. By the fifth round, everyone was covered in blood and the referee came over, obviously fed up with wading through my gore, and said: 'Mickey, you're way behind on points, you've got no chance of winning. Why not retire?' I didn't want to quit because it would mean that I would be suspended for 21 days and lose the chance of another quick fight. But Tommy couldn't staunch the bleeding and pulled me out. A lot of kids today don't seem to mind when they get stopped but I was really pissed off. I was never knocked out in my career. If they knocked me down, I'd get up – five times in one fight – and take the points defeat. To me it was a disgrace to be stopped. I knew I was a body and would never be a champion, so going the distance was my way of being a winner. My old stable-mate Ronnie Clifford once said: 'You were a tough bastard. They used to knock you down but you always got up and had a go.' It was partly pride and partly because I knew I'd get earache from Rita if I didn't. It was bad enough coming home cut up, but to lose inside the distance was unforgivable.

She didn't say too much because the money was quite good. I was paid forty pounds to fight Danny Hackett, out of which I had to pay three pounds for my return train fare to London, and thirty bob towards Tommy's ticket because he'd got two fighters on the bill. With my meals and Tommy's 25 per cent after expenses – he was very fair that way – I was left with a couple of weeks' wages for just one night's work. It may have been more painful than engineering but it paid better. Strangely enough, Danny turned up years later painting my referee pal Larry O'Connell's house, and delighted in telling him in great detail how he'd smashed me about.

I couldn't have been happier. I loved a fight and enjoyed being paid for it. I'd always made a few bob out of boxing, even as an amateur, and couldn't see much sense in getting hit for nothing. I once wore my county blazer in a tough Leeds pub called the Hussars. I was just having a tomato juice with a couple of mates when one of the locals, a bit worse for wear, came up to me and said: 'You're a boxer, eh? Let's see if you can fight.' When I refused, he accused me of being scared but I told him: 'I'm not frightened of you but I get paid to fight. I don't do it for free. If you were a decorator, you wouldn't come and paint my house for nothing, would you?' He whacked me anyway and my mates jumped in and gave him a couple. I find you can sort out most things by logical debate.

A lot of my boxing was self-taught. As a kid I would watch the lads in the booths and then go and shadow box in front of a mirror, copying the way they would turn their wrist as they punched, and how they would keep their left hand up to guard their chin. I had a bit of coaching at the Market and District Club, and at Tommy's gym when I turned pro, but the person who taught me most was an old taxi driver, Harry Hare, an ex-pro with a long broken nose. He was a diamond and taught me a lot of ringcraft, like how to roll around the ropes to get out of trouble. I also picked up a lot from sparring with Johnny Halafihi from Tonga, who twice fought Chick Calderwood for the light-heavyweight title. He was brilliant. I couldn't lay a glove on him.

Tommy had the largest stable of boxers in Europe. He never saw half of them – he'd just phone and say: 'I hope you've been training, you've got a fight.' He had some useful performers at Bradford. As well as Lloyd Walford and Johnny Halafihi, there was Phil Martin, who went on to train four British champions, Young Silky, who was ranked four, Frankie Fitzgerald, Dave Tuohy, Ronnie Clifford, who was in the top ten, Maurice Thomas, who was Alan Minter's first professional opponent, and Jim Moore. I was ranked in the top 20 but they found it difficult to decide where I should be because I'd lose to someone rated in the hundreds then beat number seven and number eleven.

Boxing gyms are functional and unglamorous places. There's no fancy decoration, just a few peeling fight posters on walls with ancient emulsion – even the mirrors always seem to be pock-marked with rust. There's usually a smell of stale sweat, old leather from the heavy bags and the gloves, and Elliman's Embrocation. Yet there's a derelict charm that old boxers still pine for. We used to get to the Farmyard about half an hour before Tommy to get the old pot-bellied stove lit to try and take the chill off the place. The stove was old and dilapidated and smoked from every orifice. There were times when we could hardly breathe in there for the fumes. We tried to stuff up the cracks with chewing gum but the smoke would just creep out from somewhere else.

We'd start with fitness work, exercises and skipping to work up a sweat. That was followed by work on the bags, after which it would be into the makeshift, sagging-roped ring for sparring. Every three minutes Tommy would shout 'Time' and give you a few instructions, then it was 'Time' again and you'd be back at it. Occasionally the landlady would come up and tell Tommy there was a phone call for him. We all knew that meant someone was needed at short notice and we'd carry on training with one eye on the door, each hoping he would get the nod. No one asked who the opponent was or how much the pay was. We were just pleased to get a fight.

One day Tommy came back and said: 'Stop sparring, Mickey, you're on at Nottingham ice rink tomorrow. I can't come down with you but there will be someone there to look after you.' That didn't bother me, especially when I found out I was on a high-quality bill and that my fight against Freddie Williams was going to be on the radio. This was the big time. Local hero Jack Bodell was up against Joe Roman, while top of the bill was a middleweight title fight between Les McAteer and Wally Swift. A promising young Scot, Ken Buchanan, was set to fight a lad from Puerto Rico.

I'm one of those people who only has to look at the sun to turn brown and having got to Nottingham early, I sat in the park with my shirt off for most of the morning while I waited for the weigh-in. When I stripped off to my shorts, ready to get on the scales, I looked in terrific condition. Freddie Williams had sent a message to say that he'd had a puncture so wouldn't be able to make the weigh-in, so I was standing around on my own waiting to be called into the ring. After a couple of minutes Ken Buchanan came over, eyeing me up and down. I'd not met him before and thought: 'What have I done to upset you, pal?' He stood about four feet from me, staring at me dead cold, and then he started shadow boxing, flashing out wicked jabs that were not that far from my face. I thought he was off his rocker. Just then a voice called 'Mickey Vann' and I climbed up into the ring, weighing in at eight stone ten. As I climbed back down the steps, Ken Buchanan was at the bottom, blocking my way. By this time, I was a bit narked and ready to have a go at him, but he just grinned and said: 'Sorry, Mickey, I thought you were the bloke I'm going to fight.' I laughed and said: 'I'm fucking glad I'm not!'

There were still several hours to go before the fight, so I killed time at the pictures, got myself a mug of tea and ate some poached egg on toast, then made my way back to the ice rink. I couldn't find the bloke who was supposed to look after me but I wasn't worried. If Tommy said someone would be there, then someone would turn up. I bandaged my hands and got one of the guys in the shared dressing-room to help me on with my gloves. I was the next fight after Ken Buchanan and as I jogged up and down on the spot and threw a few combinations to warm up, I heard the bell go for the start of his fight. Within seconds there was a huge roar from the crowd and someone was calling my name. Ken had won in the first round and as I passed him coming back, I could see he'd hardly broken sweat. 'I told you I was glad I wasn't fighting you,' I grinned.

The place was packed – it was the biggest crowd I'd boxed in front of so far, and I could feel the adrenaline kick in as I made my way into the ring. I put my towel over the top rope and took a swig of water from the house second, who I assumed Tommy had asked to look after me. I looked across the ring at Freddie Williams. He was a bloody giant! They announced the weights – Mickey Vann eight stone ten, Freddie Williams eight stone eleven and a half. I thought: 'Blimey, he must have light bones.' The ref called us to the centre for his usual pep talk. I searched Freddie's eyes for signs of cuts that might open up but there wasn't a nick on him. He didn't even have a flat nose.

The ref saw I was struggling to get my gum shield in because of my gloves and came over. 'Who's looking after you, Mickey?' I pointed to the second and explained that Tommy couldn't make it. He wasn't satisfied and asked another manager, Mac Williams, to fill in. Mac was clearly impressed by my potential that night because not long after he felt he was safe putting me in with Billy Waith, one of his fighters who went on to have 96 fights and still, as far as I know, holds the record for having the most final eliminator fights at different weights in this country.

Mind you, you could understand Mac's point of view after he'd seen me taking a battering from Williams. Freddie certainly didn't punch like a featherweight and I was up and down so many times I lost count. As Richard Dunn once memorably said, 'I was down so often I had a cauliflower arse.' The fight only lasted a few rounds and I was back in the dressing-room having five stitches in my mouth. My nose was broken and I was in a hell of a state, especially when I made the mistake of blowing my nose, which instantly closed my eyes so that I could hardly see out of them. Freddie came in and invited me for a drink. I told him I had to get my train and he said: 'OK, I'll come with you, I'm going that way.' That's the great thing about boxing. A few minutes earlier he'd been knocking me about, now he wanted to buy me a drink and help me to the station.

When I got home, I crept into bed. Rita said: 'Did you win?' and when I told her I'd been stopped, she just turned her back and snapped, 'Typical.' The next thing I remember was her scream in the morning when she saw the state of my face. It hadn't hurt during the fight and wasn't too bad on the way home, but now my whole face was swollen, bruised and throbbing like hell. Every part of me ached but that was usual the day after a fight. The pain that took longest to go away was usually the soreness on my back from sliding along the ropes. The burns used to scab over and took ages to heal.

Having been stopped, I was suspended for 21 days but on day 22 I was back in the ring, fighting Geoff Ryan in Oldham. He put me down twice, but I kept getting up and my left jab was working well that night. It was never out of his face. I broke his nose but still didn't get the rub. Another dodgy ref!

Freddie Williams was at ringside and came to see me. 'Blimey, Mickey, you're fighting again. I wish I had a manager like yours.' In fact he was managed by the great Eddie Thomas, who looked after world champions like Ken Buchanan and Howard Winstone, but I guess Eddie was a bit more careful with his lads than Tommy, so they earned less until they hit the big time. We had a chat and I said: 'Just out of interest, what did you weigh for our fight?' Freddie looked a bit sheepish and grinned: 'Nine stone ten.' In fact he never fought as a featherweight again, going on to have another 35 fights as a lightweight. I'd guessed he'd pulled a bit of a flanker but the penny only dropped later as to just how much he'd conned me and the officials. He'd missed the weigh-in because of a puncture but then walked me to the station where we caught our trains home! Still, we parted as mates, and we still are, which was more than could be said for one of my opponents.

FIVE

Don't Let Him in a Ring Again

I never kidded myself I would ever be anything out of the ordinary but I took pride in my performances, especially the two bouts where I beat guys who were highly ranked. It was a shame that by the time I was fighting, *Boxing News* had stopped giving out their Certificates of Merit. They used to present one a month for an outstanding performance and I reckon beating Mickey Lynch and Bernie Nicholls would have earned me at least one. That would have been my Lonsdale Belt, and I could have had it framed to hang with my other boxing memorabilia. As it is, I've nothing to remind me of my days as a boxer – not even a good photo of me in action.

I did once see myself in the Green Shield Stamp catalogue. There was a photo of a little lad in boxing gloves and behind him was a poster with 'Mickey Vann v. Mickey Lynch' in big letters over our photographs. We were top of the bill at the Slough Community Centre. Mickey was number seven in the country, but I'd had plenty of notice of the fight for once and worked hard, putting in loads of road work and sparring. And I guess the fact that I was returning to the place where I'd learned ballroom dancing and had a little bit of fame meant I was well up for the fight. Mickey and I went to the cinema together after the weigh-in, then had a cracking battle, which I won on points. He wanted a re-match as top of the bill in the Midlands, but Tommy had already booked me in for a six-rounder, so I missed out on a decent payday.

Mickey was another fine sportsman and we parted as mates. Bernie Nicholls was another story. He was number 11 in Britain and had already had over 30 fights when we met at the annual Jewish charity show in the CIS building in Manchester. It was an eight-rounder, with Wally Thom refereeing. I'd been selected as a body, fodder to make Bernie look impressive and set him up for a shot at bigger things. But my jab was working perfectly and I kept moving and flicking it out into his face, which started to redden. In no time I'd ripped open his right eyebrow and Wally stepped in to stop it midway through the third round. I always used to pop in to see an opponent when I won – I didn't have to do it often! – and as I entered Bernie's dressing-room the doctor was sewing him up with a big curved needle. I've never seen anyone manage to get so agitated while keeping his head perfectly still. He accused me of butting him. As if I would! I decided he wasn't interested in my consoling speech and as I beat a hasty retreat, I heard him call after me: 'I'll get you. That bastard ref. I'll get both of you.' I don't know about Wally, but he certainly got me.

A few weeks later I was in bed with the flu when Tommy Miller phoned to say I had a fight the next night at the American Army base at Burtonwood. It was Bernie again. I knew I was daft to take a grudge fight when I was feeling less than 100 per cent, but as usual I needed the money. I bumped into Bernie in the gents before the fight, hoping he might have calmed down a bit by now. No such luck. As soon as he saw me, he snapped: 'I remember you. I'm going to sort you out properly tonight.' And he did. I was down five times, but only lost on points.

Those victories over Mickey and Bernie were probably the highlight of my fight career. Mostly I would take a bout at short notice, battle gamely and end up losing the verdict. But I still loved the sport and I wanted to go on as long as I could. In my mind, I would still be boxing when I turned 40. But Rita had other ideas. She still hated the game and constantly got on to me to quit. Her nagging got more persistent when we moved house and had a lot of work to do. She wanted me to spend any spare time painting and decorating, or tidying the garden, and resented me going off training. In the end I decided the aggravation wasn't worth it and hung up my gloves. I was still only 29. I still regret finishing so soon. I'd only had a dozen fights in two years and while I might not have been that impressive, I always reckon things would have looked up if I'd kept at it. They couldn't have got much worse, that's for sure.

We missed the extra cash badly. I was running two jobs but we were still hard up. I had a little van and, after I'd finished my shifts at Towlers, I'd go out selling fruit and veg from door to door. I used to shoot down the market first thing in the morning and load up with whatever was fresh. Later I'd chuck a pair of scales in the back and go round the estates, flogging it off. That came to an end one winter morning when I came out of the market in the centre of Leeds a bit too fast. I hit a patch of ice and went into a spectacular skid, knocking down a bollard and about 20 feet of railings before smashing into the Guinness clock. The van was a write-off but it could have been worse – I managed to get it towed away before the police saw I didn't have any road tax.

With the insurance money, I went to an auction and bought myself a very cheap little Vauxhall. Rita's dad, Bill, came along to make sure I didn't buy anything that had been written off and welded back together again. He was a very good panel beater and sprayer with his own little garage and pit, so he dodged it up for me. He did a great job and I suggested that we go into business together – I'd pick up a couple of motors and sort out the mechanics, he'd tart them up and we'd split the profits. There was, of course, a snag. I knew more about brain surgery than I did about mechanics. But Bill must have thought there were advantages in the idea because he agreed. He probably thought it was the best way to keep an eye on his waster of a son-in-law, while making sure I earned a few bob so that his daughter didn't starve. He was determined I wasn't going to be a sleeping partner and set about teaching me the job. He once made me replace a complete clutch on my own while he stood and gave instructions. He never lifted a hand to help, no matter how much I cursed and struggled. He was tough but it made me learn quickly and I was soon competent. In no time I was a fully-fledged car dealer.

I started to go to all the local auctions and got to know another regular, a guy called Pat. He and I became friendly and he helped me pick out a tidy mini-van that I needed to carry my tools and timber when I did a bit of joinery. Before long we started to do quite a bit of business together. We got on really well and he introduced me to his wife. She and I got on even better. I was soon dropping in to see her twice a week when he was away looking at cars, but you just can't rely on anyone, and one afternoon he came home early. To this day I can't explain how I knew it was him, but I heard the car door slam and was in my clothes, out the window and down the soil pipe quicker than it takes to count a KO. My van was parked some way down the street, so I ducked across a couple of gardens and out through an archway, partway down the terrace. As soon as I reached the road, I started to run, yanking my keys out of my pocket as I went. I glanced back over my shoulder and saw Pat legging it after me, and he wasn't looking for a chat. I jumped in the van and to be fair to Pat, he'd chosen a beauty. It started first time. As I pulled away I heard this loud thump in the back. I didn't stop to find out what it was. I just kept my foot to the floor until I got back to the little yard, where I parked. I sat there a couple of minutes, getting back my breath, then went to see what the noise had been. Buried in the roof, up to its handle, was a Stanley hatchet.

That was the end of my car dealing and I needed to find something else pretty quick. I'd bought Rita an industrial sewing machine and she was taking in work to make some pin money, but it was slave labour and certainly didn't bring in enough to keep what had recently become a family of four with the arrival of our second son, Gary.

I have to admit I never used to worry at times like this. I always thought something would turn up. It always had for Dad and I couldn't see any reason why it wouldn't for me. Sure enough Sid Emerson, who lived down the road, said he'd pay me to help him erect a greenhouse he'd bought. He wanted me to put down the concrete base and do the brickwork. I quoted him a price that included having the concrete delivered to the site but saved a few bob by putting planks in the back of my van and having them shoot the concrete in there. As I drove along, the concrete started to settle and water was pouring out of the back of the van, getting into everything, including my rear lights. What with the hatchet dent and the hole in the roof, and the mess everywhere else, by the time I'd finished building that base the van looked like something out of a war zone.

Sid was happy with the job and recommended me to the guy who sold him the greenhouse. He put several bits of work my way and it wasn't long before I was calling myself a builder and had picked up a council contract worth a lot of money. Within months I employed 23 people, had several vans, office staff and drove round in a classy-looking Rover. I was making a terrific living and beginning to think that at last I'd found my niche in life, when the '70s building slump caught me like Mike Tyson's upper cut. I nearly went bust. I had a contract to build 60 detached, stone houses in Luddenden Foot near Halifax, some bungalows at Yeadon, and four £85,000 detached houses in Scarcroft, an up-market part of Leeds. They all went down the pan at the same time. I had to sack everyone. I also had to pay a big tax bill and at the end of it all, I still owed £20,000. Everyone told me to declare myself bankrupt, but my pride wouldn't let me. Dad wouldn't have done that. Instead, I rang my creditors and said: 'I'm going to pay you, I don't know how and I don't know when, but I will pay you.' Fortunately they all accepted my word and by working every hour God sent, I managed to pay them all in full. In addition, I bought myself a detached bungalow and paid for it.

Don't get me wrong, there was nothing heroic about it. It was a rough time and I was feeling crap. I was no longer fighting, I'd had no education and I was living on my wits and often at my wits' end. At the back of my mind I still wanted to be a somebody and the last thing I wanted to do was get a job working for someone else. Dad had never worked for anyone, and I didn't want to either. That would have been failure. As usual when things were nose-diving towards rock bottom, I thought of boxing. I still watched it on TV and went to the occasional show. I missed the banter and the camaraderie. I'd not been anything special as a fighter, but a few people still asked me for my autograph and that made me feel good.

I kept thinking that whenever I'd been involved in boxing, as an amateur or a pro, I'd been much better off than when I was out of it. I had to make some money, and I had to make it now. I knew I couldn't go back into the ring but thought I might be able to make a bob or two training other fighters. I went to see Tommy Miller, who in his usual subtle way said: 'You were never any good as a fighter, Mickey. What do you think you could teach anyone?' Tommy may not have been a diplomat but he was kind enough, and when he saw my disappointment, he added: 'Why don't you become a referee?' It wasn't something that had ever crossed my mind, but it immediately appealed to me. After all those years Tommy had at last set me off on the path to fame I'd craved. But like everything else in my life there were a few hiccups along the way.

Becoming a boxing referee is a long and arduous process. And so it should be. Once you get in the ring for real, you've got people's livelihoods and lives in your hands. The first thing is to learn the rules. I went through the book several times, committing every sentence to memory. Then I cut it into pieces and stuck it back together again with Sellotape. By the time I'd done that five or six times, I knew the rules backwards. I was summoned to a Central Area meeting at Belle Vue in Manchester, where I was tested. There were about 20 people round the table and as I walked in someone said: 'Bernie Nicholls is still looking for you, Mickey.' That made everyone laugh and relaxed me a bit. They started firing questions at me about the rules but after all my homework, I didn't have a problem.

The next stage was to judge some fights. They gave me a list of promotions that were coming up so I could pick the ones I fancied doing. I ticked them all. The idea is that you fill in a scoresheet round by round, just as if you were judging the fight for real. At the end of the fight you give your sheets to the area secretary, who compares them with the official scorecard. You not only have to get the result right, your round scores have to be similar as well. I can't have been very good, because I did that for 18 months before they were satisfied. It meant a hell of a lot of travelling, all at my own expense, and one night I even had to pay to get in. Johnny Griffin was promoting a show in Bentley, near Doncaster, and he not only insisted I paid at the door, he stuck me ten rows back from the ring. How the hell are you supposed to judge from there? Funnily enough it was the same Johnny Griffin who, years later, was among the loudest critics of Larry O'Connell after the controversial Lewis–Holyfield world heavyweight 'unification' fight. If you remember, Larry's scoring came in for a lot of criticism by those who thought Lennox had won and Johnny even had the cheek to say to a reporter that officials should be trained better.

Once the area board were happy with my scoring, they sent me to London with the recommendation that I should be tested by the British Boxing Board of Control (BBBC). Although they are the all-powerful people who control boxing in this country, at that time they were housed in a poky office in Ramillies Building in Oxford Street. I was

due up before board of control officials and three of the top referees –
Harry Gibbs, Sid Nathan and 'Doctor Death', Roland Dakin. My
appointment was for three o'clock but I was so nervous I arrived at
eleven in the morning. By the time I went in, I was literally shaking.
Harry Gibbs must have seen what a state I was in because when he
came out to fetch me, he said: 'Don't worry, Mickey. You've been a
boxer. You know what it's all about. Just take your time.' They started
to ask me questions and it went quite well until Sid Nathan started a
long rambling question about what I would do if this happens and that
happens, a woman jumps in the ring with an umbrella and the lights
go out . . . Fortunately Harry interrupted and said: 'Sid, he's not going
to referee a world championship. We only want to know if he's learned
the rules.'

I still wasn't confident when they asked me to step out of the room
for a few minutes, but when Harry came back out he had a big grin on
his face. 'Look serious when you go back in, Mickey. But you're OK.'
The rest was a bit of a blur, but I came away with the recommendation
that I should be given a trial in the ring. I still wasn't a referee – I had
to handle a couple of fights under the supervision of a star referee to
show I could put the theory into practice. The novice ref controls the
fight and scores it, but the supervising official gives the final decision,
unless there's a stoppage – that's down to the man in the ring. My two
fights were to be at the Anglo-American Sporting Club in Manchester,
a dicky-bow night. Former British, European and Commonwealth
welterweight champion, Wally Thom, was the man with my destiny in
his hands.

He gave me a bit of a pep talk beforehand and told me that if it went
the distance I was to look down at him and he would point to the
corner of the winner. The fight went quite well and I thought I'd
handled things OK. It went to a decision but when I looked down at
Wally, he was deep in conversation with the geezer next to him. It
seemed to take an eternity for him to look my way. I'd felt quite calm
during the fight, but now I was sweating and starting to feel panicky.
The crowd were a bit restive, wondering why I hadn't given a verdict.
Eventually he looked up and pointed. I went over and raised the lad's
arm, feeling increasingly worried because I thought the other fighter
had won by quite a big margin. What I hadn't realised was that while

I was looking at Wally, the fighters had switched corners for the usual handshakes with the opposing seconds. I'd given the verdict to the wrong man. The usually polite Anglo-American crowd went mad. Nat Basso, the announcer, got in the ring, shaking his head and Wally Thom was yelling: 'No, you idiot. Not him! The other one.' Completely humiliated, I had to go over and lift the other fighter's arm. I just wanted the ring to open up and let me disappear underneath. As I climbed out of the ring, I heard Nat Basso yell to the officials: 'For God's sake don't give him any more fights.' I was finished before I'd even started.

SIX

Keep on your Toes . . .

I was gutted. I'd put in a lot of effort and a hell of a lot of time to get that far and had set my heart on becoming a referee. I felt sure I had something to offer but I was already branded a flop. Fortunately the area secretary, Ricky Nicholson, came to my rescue. He'd been a football referee – the first to send off Billy Bremner – a pro golfer, and a B-grade boxing referee. He briefly became a national figure when his wig fell off in the middle of a televised football match. You would think that would have taught him a lesson, but it happened again when he was reffing a fight. Ricky was a smashing fella and a good secretary. As soon as he heard my news he phoned me to find out what had gone wrong and when I told him what had happened, he fought my corner with the Board and finally persuaded them to give me a second chance.

Wally Thom was again appointed as the star referee to assess me. I don't know if he felt a bit responsible for the previous fiasco, but he was terrific. He always used to have a little nip to steady his nerves before he got into the ring, and he decided that's what I needed. So he took me to the bar, where I had three or four, and I sailed through the fight, even managing to lift the correct arm this time. Wally sent in his recommendation that I should get a licence but the Board only make appointments every six months, so I was hanging around for ages waiting to hear the verdict. Appropriately it was Ricky who took me aside at a show and told me I was in. I was a trainee referee and licensed to handle fights up to 18 minutes long.

Now I needed experience and as so often in my life, things took an upturn at just the right time. I was given loads of fights to handle because there were only two other referees in the Central Area at the time, Harry Warner and Ron Hackett. Harry fought 97 pro fights, including beating gangster Charlie Kray at West Ham Baths. He later became area secretary and suffered a heart attack. His recovery wasn't helped by one of my cock-ups. I mixed up the dates of a fight and Harry, not long out of hospital, had to step in and handle the fight. I still feel guilty about that.

Ron was another smashing fella, who won three northern counties light-heavyweight titles and one at heavyweight, twice beating former Empire champion, Joe Bygraves. Ron took over as secretary when Harry was too ill to continue. They were both really helpful to me when I started out, giving me plenty of encouragement. Both of them were class A referees and each show needed an A and a B or a trainee B, so I worked on every bill that came up. Within a year I'd filled two score books, which meant I'd had charge of over 100 fights. I took everything that was offered, and as soon as I became a B-grade ref, I was able to accept some fights outside my own area. It was one of those that gave me my first taste of how dodgy things can become when you give an unpopular decision.

I was back in Nottingham, where Freddie Williams had given me a belting. The fight was between Alex Panaski and a lad called Danny Lawford. Panaski was a tough son of a bitch, who could do no wrong in the eyes of his Nottingham public. He gave me a tough time from the opening bell and even though I kept warning him, he still kept buggering about, trying to get away with breaking the rules. Eventually I decided enough was enough and disqualified him. The noise was incredible, with people booing and calling me every evil name they could think of. And they thought of plenty. Panaski's brother and some of his mates decided I needed a lesson in the finer points of leaning towards the local fighter and came looking for me. Luckily the police found me first and gave me an escort as far as the M1. They parked their motorbikes, blue lights flashing, in the middle of the slip-road and told me to put my foot down. I didn't need telling twice.

Maybe it was the fact that I was not fazed by being run out of town, combined with my willingness to go anywhere that gave the Board the idea of sending me to Northern Ireland. There weren't many refs over there so they put me down to handle two fights in Belfast. I've never been very political and seldom read much in the papers apart from the sports pages, so it really didn't occur to me that this could be a dangerous assignment. I was aware of the 'Irish problem' and knew that there were bombs going off and people being shot, but I reckoned that was nothing to do with me, so why should anyone want to have a go at me? I wasn't even bothered when I arrived at the Europa hotel, which I later learned was the most bombed hotel in Europe, to find it surrounded by barbed wire and sentry boxes. Eager to have a look round Belfast, I quickly unpacked, freshened up and went down to the foyer, proudly wearing my blazer with the BBC badge on the breast pocket. The badge includes quite a large Union Jack and I noticed the porter go pale when he saw it. He suggested I might like to change into something a little less ostentatious. Pointing to the badge, he said: 'There are people here who would find that an irresistible target for shooting practice!'

I began to realise this was not like being in Leeds, a feeling that was confirmed when I decided to browse around Boots, hoping to find some presents for the family. There was a long queue at one door, which I thought was probably for some special offer, so I slipped in through another entrance. I'd only just got through the door when a 15-stone security guard grabbed me and threw me out again. 'Hey,' I yelled. 'What d'ya think you're doing? I haven't nicked anything, I just want to have a look round.' He assured me that was fine, but first I had to wait in line and be frisked for weapons.

The fights went quite well. I gave Danny McAlinden the nod over Dave Fry, but ruled against the other local boxer, Dave Larmour, giving the verdict to Welshman Steve Sammy Sims, who went on to become British featherweight champion. Dave's fans were obviously disappointed, but they took the decision with a lot more grace than the people of Nottingham, and I left the arena thinking people were exaggerating the dangers of life in Belfast. I even managed to ignore the occasional sound of shots that punctuated the night, but my views changed dramatically the next morning when I reached the airport to fly home.

I got chatting to a guy and when I told him I hadn't flown much, he said: 'If you want a tip, wait here until the final call for your flight. That way you won't spend as much time in queues.' With only an overnight bag to worry about, I sat drinking coffee, feeling I was now one of the travellers 'in the know'. When the final call came, I sauntered down the slope to the security check where the guy asked me for my boarding pass. Oh shit! In my newfound, cool, 'much-travelled' mode, I'd forgotten I needed one. The security guard said: 'You'll have to go back and get it but get a move on because they won't hold the flight for you.'

I dumped my bag on his desk and started to run back up the slope towards the check-in desks. As I ran I became aware that people were diving out of my way, throwing themselves to the floor. A voice yelled: 'Stop or I'll shoot.' It didn't seem to have anything to do with me. But I stopped, anyway. When I looked back, the security guard was holding what looked like a cannon. It was pointed straight at me.

'Come down here and take this bag,' he ordered.

'But I've got to get my . . .'

'Pick up this bag.'

'But I've . . .'

'Pick it up or I'll shoot you.'

I thought he was stark, staring mad, but it was clear he wasn't kidding, so I did what I was told. I just managed to get my flight and as we headed back towards London, I understood a bit more about the incredible situation that was happening right here in Britain. I was later to get two more reminders.

I was appointed to referee the fight between Kevin Lueshing and Chris Saunders in the Docklands. As I drove down the M1 the day before the fight, the computer on my Audi kept signalling that the battery wasn't charging, but as I couldn't spot a fault, I kept going. About 20 miles from London, I ground to a halt. The car was towed away and I carried on by train. By now I was running late and was ready for something to eat. I set off on foot for the last part of the journey to the Britannia Hotel, but as I got within a few hundred yards of it there was pandemonium. People were running all over the place. Suddenly there was the sound of several thunderclaps going off at once. You could hear people screaming above the sound of acres of glass smashing. The IRA had planted a huge bomb in the heart of London.

I had to hang around for five or six hours before I was allowed to go down to the hotel. When I got there I realised that the breakdown I had been cursing all afternoon may have saved my life. If I'd been on time, I would have checked in and several of the rooms were filled with flying glass. At the very least the Audi would have suffered massive damage from the flying debris that littered the car park.

The fight for the British welterweight title was postponed until the Tuesday and moved to Bethnal Green. The champion, Chris Saunders, was unusual in modern boxing because he had a 16-win, 16-defeat record. He already had a four-round stoppage over Lueshing, who had excited a lot of people when he took the Southern area light-middleweight crown by stopping Kirkland Laing. I didn't see their first fight but this one was war. It lasted about seven minutes, with an average of one knock-down per minute. I just let them get on with it and only stepped in when Saunders was hanging over the ropes about to get a hiding. Fights don't have to last long for the customers to be happy, they just have to be real contests, and Lueshing and Saunders certainly provided that – it was voted British fight of the year.

My third encounter with the Troubles in Ireland was in Manchester. I was there for a fight a couple of days after the IRA set off a bomb in the middle of the city. It was strange to see one of England's biggest shopping centres scarred and boarded up, and no matter how much grievance they may have, I can't see how any group can justify killing and maiming innocent people, especially children.

That was all in the future. After about four and a half years as a B-grade official I was made up to A-grade, which meant I could handle any fight below British championship level. I was really into it by now and had already made up my mind that I wanted to be one of the handful of star-grade referees who take charge of the big fights. I knew it would be hard work, but I was single-minded and determined to prove myself. You have to build up to star status with a series of good performances and the turning point for me came when I was appointed to the Herol 'Bomber' Graham–Lindell Holmes fight in Sheffield. Graham's awkward style meant his fights were often untidy and could be difficult for referees, but I was well on top of things that night and called a good stoppage in the fifth round. The BBBC secretary, Ray Clarke, was at ringside and I think he earmarked me as a contender. I was invited to referee two fights in London soon after that. This was the big test. I knew Larry O'Connell and Harry Gibbs would be assessing my performance to see if I was ready to move up to star-grade.

About two weeks before the fights I went to a dinner show run by Alex Steene at a hotel near Heathrow airport. Alex was a well-known figure around the London boxing scene, where he was often seen near the heart of things wearing his dark glasses. He was born in Hunslet, the same suburb of Leeds where actor Peter O'Toole was brought up, and Alex always went out of his way to help the Leeds ex-Boxers Association. I've been a member for years and was proud to be their chairman at one stage. One of the Association's highlights each year was when we took a coachload of the lads down to a show staged by Alex's son Greg. He'd provide us with great seats and we always had a super time. This particular trip I was in high spirits, confident that before long all my hard work would pay off big time. I was at the bar during the interval when Mike Jacobs came over. He was a London-based ref, who I'd met a couple of times before. I'd always had the impression he was a bit full of himself. Still, he'd come for a chat, so I gave him the benefit of the doubt. After a bit he said: 'You're up for star-grade, aren't you? How long have you been reffing?' When I told him it was eight years, he replied: 'You've no chance. I was 17 years before I got my star. They're just going through the motions.'

That put a damper on my evening and as we rode back to Yorkshire I kept thinking about what he'd said. As the miles slipped away, I got myself into a bit of a state that the Board would expect me to take a day off work and travel to London at my own expense, when they had no intention of promoting me. Things were no better when I got indoors. I tossed and turned all night. By the time I got up I was seething and got straight on the phone to Ray Clarke to tell him I wasn't going to bother. I told him what Mike Jacobs had said and let him know that I wasn't prepared to play silly buggers. When they were willing to consider me seriously, they could give me a call.

I was in full flow when Ray broke in: 'Mickey, don't take any notice of what Mike said. We'll watch how you handle the fights and if we think you're good enough, you will get your star-grade. It all depends on how you do. There's no question of us making up our mind beforehand and it certainly doesn't matter how long you've been a ref.

If you are good enough, you'll get it.' That calmed me down and I decided to take his word and see how things turned out.

My first fight was between Rudi Pika and Glenn McCrory. I gave it to Pika on points, only the second defeat of McCrory's career. I see a lot of Glenn these days as he's a resident pundit for Sky Sport's boxing coverage and I often wonder if he realises it was me who ruled against him. Then I took Gary Mason against Louis Perguard, who retired in the fourth round. Both of those went well but I still didn't get a decision on my upgrade. Instead I was sent to the Isle of Man, where Sid Nathan was going to watch me and report back. I was a bit nervous because Sid had the reputation of never recommending anyone. Sitting at ringside, waiting to go on, I noticed that Norman Wisdom was just behind me. We got talking and he told me he used to be a decent amateur boxer. That took my mind off things and the two bouts I reffed went well. A few weeks later I was in charge of a fight near home in Morley. I disqualified a lad and as I climbed out of the ring, Nat Basso, the Central Area chairman who had said I should never get another fight after my cock-up with Wally Thom, came over. I wondered if he was going to criticise my decision. Instead he told me I'd got my upgrade. I was chuffed to bits. At 42 years of age I was the youngest star-grade referee. There was a lot of handshaking and backslapping. But when I got home, Rita greeted the news with: 'I suppose I'll see even less of you now.'

To hell with her. She couldn't spoil my satisfaction and that old grin was plastered across my face for weeks. I was now able to referee title fights and before long I was in the ring for my first championship bout between Langton Tinago and Tony Brooks in the Granada Studios in Manchester, where they battled it out for the Commonwealth lightweight belt. I was as nervous as hell, but it wasn't too difficult a fight and I thought I did OK. Tinago was badly cut but came back to win. I did another of his fights later on and was due to take a third, but it was called off because he was HIV positive.

I was walking tall – well, as tall as someone who's 5 ft 9 in. can walk – and I have to admit that for a while I found the small club shows a bit difficult; delusions of grandeur, I suppose, but that soon passed. As I was working my way up, I entered the ring thinking 'How would a star ref handle this fight?' and tried to act accordingly. Now I have a different approach, whatever fight I'm in charge of. Three weeks after the world heavyweight clash between Lewis and Bruno, I was at a small show in Hull. And believe me, I was keyed up for it. I didn't want to give anyone the chance to say that my standards had slipped. I want fight fans to be able to notice the difference between a star referee and the rest. It may sound big-headed but, while the fans are watching a fight, I like to think they are aware of me and I want to perform at my best every time.

My promotion to star-grade was probably the last straw for my marriage. I knew Rita was fed up with my refereeing. She'd been OK at first, but gradually she became more and more bitter because I was always out. Her resentment grew when I started to travel abroad for fights. I really don't think she expected me to succeed, but I'd taken to it like a Jock to haggis. I was in my element and quite prepared to put up with some earache at home if it meant I could reach the top. Mind you, I'd underestimated just how far Rita would go to try and scupper things for me.

Like all marriages, we had good times, not so good times and what-the-hell-am-I-doing-here? times. Mostly we just muddled through, getting on with making a living and bringing up the boys. Rita always seemed a bit suspicious of me, even when I was behaving myself. Once, when we took the boys to Bridlington for the day, she became convinced I was up to no good, even though I was totally innocent. It was a beautiful day and the lads were having fun on the beach, so I suggested that instead of going back early, we should hang on and book into a B&B. She agreed so I went off to find somewhere to stay. The first couple of places were booked up, but one of them suggested a place just round the corner. I rang the bell and was stunned when Nina opened the door. I hadn't seen her since that eventful day of our broken engagement and I could tell she was as startled as I was. But she didn't slam the door in my face and after a 'How are you? What are you doing here?' chat, I explained I had Rita and the boys with me and we needed a place to stay for the night.

Nina was very relaxed about it but when I got back to Rita I somehow couldn't tell her who owned the boarding house I'd booked into. We stayed on the beach another couple of hours and I realised I was going to have to break the news. Rita exploded. 'I'm not staying with that woman. You either find somewhere else or we go home.' I explained we couldn't because I'd already paid. When we arrived at Nina's the atmosphere was decidedly chilly, although it thawed a bit as the evening went on. Rita gave me another earbashing when we got in our room and all the time we were there she never let me out of her sight.

Rows were now common in the Vann household as Rita and I drifted apart. Usually they were connected with boxing and the amount of time I was spending away from home. To be honest, I became numbed to the arguing, but Rita's next move was much more significant and could well have created my unique style of moving round the ring. People have often commented that I move differently from other refs. It's important to be able to weave around the ring, making sure you don't get in the boxers' way while still being close enough to the action to see what's going on. When people ask how I developed my style of shuffling on my toes, I say it came from my time as a boxer or as a ballroom dancer. In reality it was probably because I didn't want the crowd to see my bum.

I've always prided myself on my appearance in the ring. I like to be immaculate from my dicky bow to the Union Jack socks I usually wear. (I don't wear them in Ireland or Argentina – I may not be the brightest lad in the world but I'm not kamikaze.) One night as I was climbing through the ropes, one of the seconds said: 'Mickey, your trousers are split.' I put my hand behind me and sure enough, the back seam had gone. There was no time to change and I didn't have a spare pair of black trousers with me anyway. My mind was racing. I decided that if I pinched the trousers between the cheeks of my backside and moved very carefully, I might just get away with it. Then it hit me: 'What if there's a knock-down and I have to bend over and count?' Luckily there were no counts and I got through with my dignity intact.

When I reached home, I asked Rita to mend my trousers and thought no more about it until the night of my first world championship fight. I was a judge when Dennis Andries defended his WBC and British light-heavyweight belts against Tony Sibson, and as I sat down a steward said: 'Mickey, you've lost a button.' When I looked, there wasn't a single button on my dinner suit jacket. As Oscar Wilde would have said if he'd been there, to lose one button is a misfortune, to lose the bleedin' lot is decidedly fishy. The penny dropped – Rita had cut them all off.

This was war and I have to admit, I lost several of the battles. By now I was wearing black boxer shorts under my trousers just in case, and would check buttons and seams before I set off, but Rita still managed to pull a few strokes to get back at me. Before one fight I put my scorecard into my back pocket and it slipped straight down my trouser leg on to the canvas – she'd cut the lining out of all my pockets. I arrived at one fight to find my patent leather shoes had no laces and I had to referee with brown laces in black shoes – so much for the smart image. And when I went to assess Dave Parris for his star-grade, I discovered she'd cut the whole of the lining out of my jacket.

Dave's assessment was cursed all round – I nearly missed it altogether. He was down to referee a couple of fights at Wembley and when I got off the tube I found myself in the middle of a huge crowd, waiting for the doors of the Arena to open. I persuaded the doorman that it was important I got in straight away. I was a bit surprised when I saw that the seats were set up theatre style, but sat there for a bit, reading the paper, waiting for someone I knew to arrive. After about half an hour I started to get a bit anxious and asked one of the usherettes where the ring was.

'The ring?' she asked.

'Yeah, the boxing ring,' I said.

'There's no ring here. There's a big pop concert on tonight. Have you tried next door at the conference centre?'

I scampered round there to find the anxious-looking Dave pacing up and down wondering where the hell I'd got to.

Perhaps the worst thing Rita did to me was for a fight I handled in Liverpool. At that time I was running a skip-hire business and quite often when she knew I had to get to boxing, Rita would insist she needed the car, leaving me to drive to the venue in my skip truck, usually still loaded with skips. That was humiliating enough, but as I drove home from the fight on Merseyside it started to rain and as soon as I switched on the wipers, there was a dreadful screeching noise. Rita had taken the rubber blades out, leaving the metal arms to scrape uselessly across the windscreen.

As you can imagine, by then we were not getting on too well. It wasn't all Rita's fault. I'm not easy to live with and I pulled a few strokes that upset her, like buying a new bungalow without telling her. I'd become fed up with her always moaning about where we lived and thought I'd shut her up. My 'thoughtfulness' might have been more appreciated if I'd let her look at the place before buying it. As it was, her first view was of a jungle of a garden and a house that needed a lot of work on it. She knew she'd be the one who had to do most of the sorting out and she let me know she was pissed off.

I was trying to keep out of her way as much as possible and found myself a lock-up garage to use as an office and bolthole. I set it up really comfortably with a bed-settee and other bits and pieces of furniture, and it soon became a sanctuary where I could sit and have a quiet smoke and a can of beer. The lock-up was near the local Makro store where my younger son, Gary, had a job as a trolley boy. I used to pop in there for petrol and it was there I met Karen. She was working behind the counter and I took a shine to her straight away. She was 28 years old, and about 5 ft 5 in. tall with long blonde hair and a great figure. Even though she didn't have much cash at the time, she always aspired to quality, wanted to be dressed fashionably and to look at her best. She cared what people thought about her and liked it when I flattered her. Each time I dropped in, which became increasingly frequently, we'd chat a little longer and finally I started to go round the back and sit in the office and talk to her while she worked. Over the weeks she started to tell me her troubles. She was married to a Muslim. They had a young son and the culture-clash was causing her all kinds of problems. She always walked around with her eyes cast down, as though she was frightened to look the world in the face.

I was doing some building work at Reynold's newsagents in Dixon Lane, near where Karen lived, and found myself looking out for her, hoping she would walk past. One day she waved and called out that she'd won £50 on the premium bonds. I climbed down from the scaffold and went over for a chat. I was thrilled for her because she never had much cash of her own. 'Why don't you and me go out one evening and celebrate?' I asked her. 'That would be nice but I can't, Mick. I'm married and it wouldn't be right.' It was then I realised how much I'd come to like her and how much I wanted to take our friendship beyond just an occasional chat. But she wouldn't be persuaded and my whole mood changed as I watched her walk home. I was still feeling sorry for myself when I heard her call out: 'Mick, OK. Why not?' She told me later that when she got indoors her husband had given her grief and she'd thought: 'What the hell.'

Our first date was 4 November, Mischievous Night! She was 16 years younger than me, but that didn't seem to matter. We drove up to the local park and sat chatting for an hour or so. I was strangely nervous when I asked her if she'd see me again and was delighted when she said yes. This went on for a while and, as it does, eventually one thing led to another and we became lovers. Rita was beginning to get suspicious because I was away from home even more than usual. She began to wonder why I was pricing more jobs than ever but getting less work. She got wind of the fact that I was seeing a blonde who worked at the Makro garage and decided to try and catch us together. Luckily for me she didn't know that Karen only worked there at weekends, and was following the wrong blonde.

I became quite ingenious at covering my tracks, but one escape was pure luck. To this day I don't know why I asked Gary if I could borrow his car for the evening but, having parked mine some distance away, I picked up Karen in his and drove to one of our favourite spots, overlooking the park. It was a cold night and as we started to warm things up, the windows began to steam over. Two or three cars came and went but I was too engrossed to take much notice. It was only later that I found out one of them had been Rita looking for me. But she'd driven away when she'd seen the car, thinking our Gary was up to no good.

The car was a bit cramped and uncomfortable for what I had in mind, so I rigged the door on the lock-up so that it could be closed from the inside while the padlock was still done up on the outside. Anyone looking at it would be given the impression no one was there, but often Karen and I were inside sharing a bottle of wine. Very cosy.

After several years with hardly any romance in my life, of constant bickering and indifference, I suddenly felt alive again. Karen wanted to be with me and I looked forward to seeing her. I missed her when she wasn't around. We would go off for the day, where no one knew us, and where we could relax and just enjoy each other's company. I loved to buy her presents, and when she passed her driving test I gave her a white Suzuki Swift. Her old man must have thought she was very thrifty to be able to save up and buy all these things – especially the car.

We even managed to get a holiday together. Her husband never went away, so she booked to go to Newquay with her son. Obviously I couldn't stay at the same hotel because her lad would recognise me, but I managed to get a room in a hotel almost opposite. He also knew my Tonka, so I had to work out how I was going to get there. Fortunately a good mate, Mark Coulson, agreed to lend me his XR3 while he had the van. Then there was the small matter of what to tell my wife.

I arranged for someone to phone me at home and rhubarb down the phone. When I hung up I said: 'That was a job. I've got to go to Italy for the week.' Normally Rita would take me to the airport so I said Mark was going to drive me there, and covered up the fact that he was taking the van by saying he needed it for some jobs. It was all a bit complicated, but Rita was used to me dashing off and didn't ask too many questions. She was probably glad to see the back of me for a while.

Karen and I had a great week. I had the days to myself to potter about and see a bit of Newquay, then in the evening when her lad was asleep, I'd nip in and see Karen, slipping out again around four in the morning. I was in a great mood as I drove home the following Saturday morning, foot on the floor and singing along with the radio. My mind was still on the good time I'd had when I came to a traffic jam. The realisation that the car in front of me had stopped broke through my daydream too late. I slammed on the brake but still caught the back of it with a sickening crunch and smashing of glass. Luckily there wasn't too much damage and no one was hurt, but I still had to pay for both cars to be repaired. What with that, the petrol, hotel and a few bob of my 'Italian earnings' for Rita, that holiday in Cornwall was probably the most expensive I've ever had. But it was worth it.

Whenever you are in a relationship outside your marriage, you're always more dissatisfied at home and that was happening to me in a big way. Karen couldn't get away very often and sometimes when she could, I wasn't able to make an excuse and see her. That would give me the hump and I'd be even more moody at home. It was a vicious circle. Because she and I were getting on so well, it highlighted the chasm that had opened up between Rita and me. I decided I had to get out, but first I needed somewhere to live. I started to tuck a few bob aside and when I had about a grand, I found myself a house in Whitehall Road in Leeds. With a bit of imaginative form-filling, I managed to persuade a building society to give me a mortgage and picked up the keys just before Christmas.

Christmas was always a fraught time in our house. Rita seemed to get worked up into a state whenever there was a holiday, probably because she wanted it to go well. But it always ended up with her telling me what I could and couldn't do, and that would inevitably lead to a row. This year was no different and we had a right set to on Christmas Eve. Gary had retreated into his room out of the way and I decided now was as good a time as any to leave. I went to my room and packed a few things in a case. I popped my head round Gary's door:

'I've had enough, son. I'm going,' I said.

'Where will you go?'

'I've bought a house in Whitehall Road.'

He looked at me, stunned. A dozen thoughts flashed across his eyes before he said: 'Can I come?'

'Of course you can. Get packed.'

He threw some clothes into a bag and followed me into the kitchen. Before Rita could say anything, I said: 'I'm off. I can't put up with this any more.' I picked up my case and as I reached the door, I added: 'And Gary's coming with me.'

We climbed into the van and in the mirror I caught my last view of my marriage – Rita giving me a V-sign and yelling obscenities.

The house in Whitehall Road wasn't ready to live in yet, but fortunately friends of mine, Kath and Malcolm, were going away for the holiday and said Gary and I could stay at their place. They left us plenty of food, fruit, chocolates and drink, and for Christmas lunch we tucked into Bernard Matthews turkey portions. On Boxing Day we started to sort out the house and it was ready to move into before Kath and Malcolm came back. My main feeling was relief. I was back in charge of my life. I could see Karen whenever she could get away, and I could travel the world for my boxing without aggravation.

SEVEN

Sit Me in the Middle

If I had a fiver for every person who has said 'Can I carry your bag?' when they heard I was off to some exotic place to referee a fight, I'd be living the life of a lottery winner. It is a great life, especially as I'm a free spirit and love to travel. I've been to more than 30 different countries at someone else's expense and I'm hoping to fit in a few more before I retire. I've enjoyed more than my share of luxury, but you shouldn't get carried away with the idea that it's all silk sheets and room service. Boxing referees have to fend for themselves much of the time and you've got to be able to flannel and bullshit your way through problems, and be ready to rough it at times. You also have to learn to deal with people who will be your best mate until you give a decision against their fighter. Then you are a pariah, and if you expect a car to pick you up to take you to the airport after you've given the verdict against the local hero, you'll miss a lot of planes.

When you read of the millions of dollars washing around in boxing don't run away with the idea that referees are paid huge fees and given unlimited expenses. When I first started, we got a lump sum in Swiss francs to cover everything. That's changed now and we get an allowance over and above the fee, but a lot of mine goes on my trip to Heathrow because my ticket inevitably starts from London. If you are not careful, you end up out of pocket. That was certainly true on my first trip, which was to Copenhagen as a judge on the WBC lightweight international title bout between Gert Bo Jacobsen and Felipe Julio. John Coyle was reffing the European heavyweight title on the same bill, so naturally we stayed together and went to the hotel bar for a

drink. He had a spirit and I had a whisky and orange, and I held out
a handful of cash for the barman to take what he needed. I've never
been quick with figures and even though I've lived in Yorkshire for
about 40 years, I still don't count every penny. But it did strike me that
I'd just parted with a lot of cash. John Coyle did a quick sum and said:
'Blimey, Mickey, we'll make these drinks last. They've cost seventeen
quid.'

Some of the destinations leave something to be desired, too. The
bleakest place I've ever been is Neuuppin, which was then in East
Germany. It was like a scene in one of those Len Deighton cold war spy
films: grey, desolate and barren. You hardly saw a child around the
place, and the adults were given a vodka ration to help wipe out the
misery of their existence. The fight was held in a draughty old school
hall that was lit by sparse gaslights, so you went from dark to light to
dark again. Everything and everyone seemed depressed and
impoverished, yet my taxi, a beaten-up old Skoda, had the latest
computerised route-finder equipment used to avoid traffic jams. Given
the lack of cars, it seemed a bit of an indulgence.

Not long after that, WBU president, Jon Robinson, asked me to go
to Abidjan in the Ivory Coast. I had to look it up on the map but I was
keen to go to a part of the world I'd not seen before. Seldom have I
come across such stark contrasts. Sections of the city were extremely
wealthy with huge, American-style apartment blocks, while in other
areas there was abject poverty, with sewage in the streets. When I went
round the back of one shop I found a shantytown with little girls, no
more than ten years old, offering themselves as prostitutes. The hotel
was very basic and it was the only place in the world where I've had
stomach trouble. I'm usually careful about what I eat, but I was very
sick that trip. I spent some time by the hotel pool, making sure I wasn't
too far from the gents, and my already troubled insides turned to water
when I was attacked by what I thought was a foot-long dinosaur. I was
chatting to Andre Grutenburg, one of the judges, when this lizard leapt
on my chest and dug its claws into me. I've never moved so fast and
the only thing louder than my squawk was Andre's laughter.

When I felt well enough to do a bit of sightseeing, I was given a
police escort to make sure I wasn't mugged. I asked my guard if there
was a lot of crime. 'Oh no, sir,' he replied, with a ghoulish grin. 'We

have ways of persuading people to obey the law.' He then gave me a gruesome example of their technique, based on a supermarket robbery a couple of days before we arrived. 'We soon caught the three guys who did it,' he assured me. 'But they wouldn't tell us what they had done with the money. My superior questioned them. He is not a patient man and soon he hit the one on the left hard about the head. But still they wouldn't speak, so he took a spike and hit the one on the right. Then they told us.' I looked at him to see if he was joking but he seemed serious. I said: 'Do me a favour – if I step out of line, sit me in the middle!'

There are times when I envy film stars, pop singers and professional footballers, who have all the boring travel details taken care of and only have to turn up at the VIP lounge. A lackey handles the luggage, tickets and even their passport, and you wonder if they realise the kind of aggravation that's involved in international travel. Getting to the fight can be the hardest part of the job, as I discovered when I was appointed to referee the mandatory WBC world lightweight title fight between Leavander Johnson and Miguel Angel Gonzalez in Mexico. The tickets were supposed to arrive via Federal Express, ready for me to fly out on the fourth of August. That made things a bit tight because it was the day after I was due in Bristol to do the Ross Hale–Hugh Forde British welterweight championship. As I set out to drive to the West Country, the tickets still hadn't arrived for a flight due to leave Leeds–Bradford airport at seven o'clock the next morning to connect with my plane from Heathrow.

I phoned Federal Express from Bristol and was told they had the tickets but hadn't been able to deliver them because they needed a signature. I did the fight – Forde put up a good show before being stopped by a big punch in the seventh round – then drove like Michael Schumacher back to Leeds. It took me some time to find the FedEx office in Morley, only to be told that they couldn't let me have the tickets without some ID. I raced back home to get my Board of Control licence, picked up the tickets and managed to snatch a couple of hours sleep before the taxi arrived to take me to the airport.

I started to relax once I was on the plane. I was going to be the first Englishman to referee in Mexico and I was sure I was in for a cracking bout. I'd seen Johnson fight in Las Vegas and rated him highly. He was unbeaten in over 25 fights, most of them won by knockouts, and had earned the right to be named as mandatory contender. But Gonzalez was the champion and no mug. He was unbeaten in over 30 fights, with a high percentage of stoppages. This was the kind of fight referees love. I grabbed some kip on the plane and looked forward to a night to remember.

I flew into El Paso and looked for the guy who was supposed to meet me. No one stood there with my name on a board. I waited. And waited. Three hours went by and I began to wonder what the hell I could do. I'd only got a few dollars on me and about a hundred quid in sterling, which I planned to change once I was in Mexico. I'd left my driving licence at home so I couldn't hire a car. And I didn't have the promoter's phone number. I used my few precious dollars to phone the British Board secretary, John Morris, in London but he couldn't find anyone to help.

The only thing I could do was take a taxi. But could I persuade a cabby to take an unknown Englishman, who had only a handful of dimes and some English money, about 50 miles in the middle of the night? By now I'd been at the airport for six hours and the place was deserted except for a couple of security guards who made me a cup of coffee and told me there was a service station nearby where the owner would change my pounds. I wouldn't say the guy took advantage of my situation, but the exchange rate smacked more of Dick Turpin than Thomas Cook. Still, now armed with dollars, I managed to persuade a taxi driver that nothing less than the future of boxing depended on me getting to my hotel that night. He was clearly convinced, or maybe the promise of a big tip swayed him.

I sat in the back of the cab seriously pissed off. I became almost apoplectic when we reached the border and the guard insisted on searching my luggage. The driver sidled up to me and said: 'If you don't slip him something, he'll unpack it all and drop it all over the road. We'll be here for ages.' I felt like taking the guard's gun and ramming it up his jacksie but decided the easiest way was to give him ten dollars.

We reached Juaréz about nine at night. I'd had little sleep for what now seemed like days and my usual sunny disposition was edgy to say the least. I asked the taxi driver to go to the biggest hotel in town, where they told me the boxing party was in the Holiday Inn opposite. I paid off the cab and went to look for the promoter. I'm not a prima donna, and I hate arrogant people who think they can throw their weight around just because they are in the public eye, but I felt justified in letting him know I wasn't happy. 'You left me in that fucking airport for fucking hours,' I started, turning the air blue as I told him exactly what I thought of his organisational skills.

I was just running out of expletives when the receptionist told me they didn't have a room for me. I soon thought of a few more. 'That's fucking it. I'm going home. You can stick your fight up your arse!' By this time I'd got his attention and within a couple of minutes I was taken to my room – the bridal suite. As the porter put my bags down, he said apologetically: 'Please, sir, don't unpack or take off your clothes. There is a wedding reception in the ballroom and we shall have to move you before the bride and groom come here.' Two hours later I was dragged half asleep into another room and collapsed on top of the bed until late the next morning. That couple don't know how close they came to having three in a bed on their first night.

A good sleep cheered me up but the drama continued when I went for a walk with Bob Logist, one of the judges from Belgium. We went round the market, where there were flies all over the meat and fruit, and rats everywhere. I was sauntering along behind Bob, starting to think about the fight, when I saw three guys approaching him. One went to his left, another to his right, while the third bumped into him and slipped his hand into his pocket. I shouted out: 'Look out Bob, they're dipping you!' and went to grab the guy. The other two started back towards us and Bob said: 'Leave it, Mickey. I've still got my wallet.' I was so frustrated by the journey the day before that I was ready to have a go but Bob held me back. We went back to the hotel and related the story. 'You were lucky you didn't fight,' the doorman told us. 'They would have knifed you without a second thought.'

In the end the boxing made all the hassle worthwhile. The fight was a cracker, voted as runner-up for world fight of the year, and it so impressed the guys at Granada TV that they bought the rights and screened it twice over here even though it was between two foreigners. The fight was held in a bullring, packed to the rafters with a fantastically noisy crowd. Johnson and Gonzalez were well up for it and it was a war from the opening bell despite the searing heat. At the end of the first round they just wouldn't stop and I had to jump in with such force to separate them that Gonzalez went down on his backside. I stopped the fight in the eighth round in Gonzalez's favour. My feet were raw with blisters from having to move around so much. I was full of admiration for the gutsy display by both fighters and proud to have been part of such a great sporting occasion.

Because I'm divorced and always willing to fly off at a moment's notice, I often get the call to go to the other side of the world. It means I experience a lot of different cultures and some strange eating habits, which is how I ended up eating cheese and tomato sandwiches in Zambia one Christmas, and grilled bananas in Thailand another.

The Zambia trip was for the WBC light-heavyweight international title between Ray Aquaye jnr and Lotte Mwale, one of the best fighters to come out of Africa. It was held in Lusaka two days before Christmas. The hotel was nothing special. There were huge spiders and creepy-crawlies in the bathroom, which meant I daren't have a bath for the whole time I was there. The window was jammed open, allowing all kinds of insects to fly in, especially mosquitoes, so whenever I was in the room at night I had the light switched off. It got worse when I went to the restaurant for something to eat. There was a huge plate of what looked like sparrows' legs. I took one look at it and decided to stick to cheese and tomato. You can't muck that about too much.

Local civil unrest meant bodyguards accompanied us everywhere we went. 'Don't carry a camera, it will be snatched from round your neck,' they warned. At first my plans to do some shopping looked likely to be frustrated because we were only allowed to change a tenner into local currency. Apparently it was a serious offence to change more on the black market, but fortunately the colonel who was put in charge of our security managed to do a deal for me. It's not what you know . . .

The supervisor from Ghana obviously knew more than I did, because he stayed at home and I had to take on his job as well. With all the problems, especially over money, I was worried we might not get our fee and told the promoters that I wanted all the officials paid in US dollars before the fight could go ahead. 'Oh, Mr Vann. That is impossible. I will give you a cheque.' Now I knew I had a problem.

Don't get me wrong, boxing promoters are nearly all honest guys – trust me, I'm a doctor! – but I learned early on that cheques are not a good idea, especially if you are going to be flying home straight after the fight. I dug in my heels – no dollars, no fight. He must have got the message because he eventually relented. Even then he had to get special permission from the president to draw the dollars out of the bank.

The fight was part of a huge celebration weekend, which the whole country seemed to be joining in. It included a big football match between the Lusaka Red Devils and a team from Algeria in the African Cup. They'd never reached the final before and had never hosted a world title fight, so this was some party. We were invited along to the match and it was an extraordinary experience. I thought Leeds United fans were noisy and partisan, but they are as polite as a croquet crowd compared to the Lusaka supporters that day.

Going to the match meant I was unable to do my customary check on the ring. Even after the game – the Red Devils lost – I still wasn't able to go to the arena because there was a panic back at the hotel that needed my attention. Aquaye's manager was saying his boxer wouldn't fight unless he got more money. I pointed out that he had a contract and should honour it, but it cut no ice with him. We talked about it for a while and finally I decided to stop fannying about: 'Look, pal, you're just being a greedy bastard. If you wanted more, you should have negotiated it at the beginning instead of trying to blackmail people now.' He looked a bit startled but was still shaking his head, so I pushed a finger into his chest and added: 'If this fight doesn't go ahead there are going to be a hell of a lot of unhappy people out there, and believe me, I'll make sure every one of them knows it's you who's screwed up and why. I don't rate your chances of getting out alive, do you?' He agreed to fight.

I finally reached the arena about 45 minutes before the fight was due to go out live on TV. The place was already heaving and I quickly realised that I was the one they were likely to string up, because there was no way I could allow the bout to start. When I climbed in the ring the ropes were fine, but as soon as I stamped my foot I discovered they had put the canvas straight on top of tongue-and-groove wood planking. It was solid. Anyone going down on that could hit his head and be seriously hurt. I grabbed the nearest official: 'Where the fuck's the safety mat?' I yelled. He looked blank. It turned out they didn't have one. My first thought was to quietly get a cab to the airport before the fans realised that their cup final defeat was only the first disappointment of the day. Then I had a brainwave. 'Quick, take me to the offices.' We raced to the nearest office at the back of the arena, shifted the furniture out of the way, ripped up the carpet and dragged it to the ring. We just got it down and the canvas replaced before the cameras went live.

The fight went well and there was pandemonium in the hall, so you can imagine my surprise at the end of the fourth round when I went to collect the judges' scores and found Roy Ankra fast asleep. The former Empire featherweight champion was clearly riveted by the action. I managed to wake him up without anyone noticing and he quickly scribbled 10–9 on his card and handed it over. Fortunately it didn't matter in the end, because I stopped the fight in the eighth round. I worked with Roy again on a Donnie Hood WBC international fight in Glasgow. It was staged outdoors on a freezing night with the rain beating down relentlessly. Even with the canopy over us, the rain was running down my back and soaking me. My teeth were chattering with the cold. I remembered to check on Roy to make sure he was with us, but even he couldn't sleep that day.

When I got to Lusaka airport the morning after the fight, Christmas Day, I still had a load of local cash that I wasn't supposed to have. I went straight to the duty-free, thinking I could spend it on some presents for Karen. I always tried to take her something back from each trip if I could. She liked nice clothes, so I would hunt around for something a bit different. Or I would buy her some jewellery; a bracelet or some earrings. I'd tuck them away in my suitcase so Rita wouldn't see them, then smuggle them out the first chance I got and give them to Karen. At that stage we would meet up for at least a short time almost every day I was at home. Her sister knew about us and would let us meet at her house, and she would always pass on a message for me. With her husband working nights, I was able to phone Karen when I was abroad but I had to be a bit careful to work out the time difference so I didn't drop her in it. I think she told her husband that she bought the clothes and jewellery herself, but she didn't have to lie this time, because I was out of luck – the duty-free shop wouldn't take their own currency. I ended up buying a lot of tat at one of the airport shops and dumping it on a bench. I arrived back at Heathrow in the early hours of Boxing Day only to find there were no flights, buses or trains to Leeds. I spent the day sitting round the airport until eight the next morning. Happy Christmas, Mickey.

I was hanging around Heathrow again before I flew to Thailand for the WBU flyweight championship between Pisnurachank Sornipichai and challenger Daniel Ward from South Africa. Trying to save a few bob on expenses, I took the coach to London but that meant I had to wait at the airport for seven hours before the thirteen-hour flight to Bangkok. Over the years I've become quite good at whiling away the time. I drink a lot of coffee, mooch around the shops, chat to people, drink more coffee and read all the papers. I really don't mind it too much.

The driver who met us in Bangkok took us to the Blue Wave hotel, which was first class by any standards. The only snag was that we only stayed there two days. Then we were packed into a tiny propeller plane, about the size of a Spitfire, together with a load of sheep and cows. After a smelly, bumpy three-hour flight, we were transferred to an ancient bus for another hour and a half, rattling through the clammy forests until we arrived at what is best described as a campsite. Round the edges were a number of small chalets where we were to stay. Mind you, that was luxury compared to the fighters, who were training in little huts in the middle of the jungle halfway up the side of a hill.

Our own accommodation was basic enough. A sign said there was a swimming pool, but it was no more than a pond with so much scum on the surface that I wouldn't have washed mud in it. Inside my hut there was a single bed with an eiderdown and sheets that looked newly laundered. The only other things in the room were two coat hooks for a wardrobe, a television showing a fight, and insects. Thousands of insects. There were insects everywhere you looked. And I hate insects. I tried to change the channel on the TV but there was nothing else on. I discovered later that all the electricity came off a generator and the voltage was so low, they could only run programmes off a central video. They'd selected the boxing tape especially for us. In the bathroom there was a toilet and a hole in the floor with a tap above it, which made do as a shower. As I stood having a pee, I looked up and saw a column of ants marching along near the ceiling and out through a hole further down the wall. I was there for four days and this procession never stopped. I never did find out if it was an endless army of ants or one group going round and round.

The team for the fight was the English supervisor, Danny Gill, referee Bruce McTavish, one-time winger for the all-conquering New Zealand rugby team, and the judges: Des 'No Neck' Bloyd, a 5 ft 8 in. solid lump of a man, who never stopped laughing and ate anything that stood still; Frank Skilbred, a quiet American from Florida; and me. Our Boxing Day meal was taken outside, round an open fire. We were each given a spike with a banana on it, which we had to cook in the flames. This simple dish tasted better than it sounds and I wasn't too unhappy when I said goodnight and went off to bed. With so many creepy-crawlies around, I decided to sleep in my clothes. Then I realised the light switch was on the opposite wall to the bed, so I switched off the light, took off a shoe and beat a path across the floor till I reached the bed and jumped in shuddering.

The next morning there was a knock on my door around seven o'clock and when I opened it, a little old Thai man stood there with a cup of coffee. He was less than five ft tall and at least 80 years old, and had walked about a quarter of a mile from the kitchen, so the coffee that hadn't been spilled was cold. Some of the party started to complain about the conditions but I reckoned that old man summed it all up – it might have been primitive by our standards, but everyone was doing their best to make us feel as welcome as they could. All it really did was emphasise how lucky we are at home.

That was underlined when we got talking to the woman who owned the place. She had two daughters aged seven and twelve, both working around the camp. They were quiet, rather shy, polite girls. Yet their mum told us that within six months the older daughter would be sold to people in Bangkok, who would turn her into a prostitute. The money, a hundred dollars, was a year's wages to her parents. They seemed to accept it as a fact of life, but I couldn't get my head round a mother selling her innocent daughter like that. We had a whipround and gave the woman a hundred dollars, saying we hoped she would look after her daughter, but I've often wondered since if she just took that as a bonus and that kid is now working the streets or brothels in Bangkok.

The fight was to be held in a car park in a nearby village. To me it seemed miles from anywhere, but there must have been 20,000 people packed into the makeshift arena. There were about 50 sponsors – the promoter pays the TV company to cover the fight in Thailand – and before the main fight, each one presented gifts to the two boxers. It took nearly three quarters of an hour while each sponsor handed over money, gold chains strong enough to walk a dog, or jewellery. I stood there and thought: 'Now I know why they are willing to lock themselves away halfway up a mountain.'

It was a brilliant fight, with Sornipichai looking set to lose his crown until he produced a big finish and stopped Ward in the 11th round. Afterwards there was a massive banquet with a band and endless food. It was great – until they brought us back down to earth by taking us back to the camp.

New Year's Eve in Bangkok was an anticlimax because there were only one or two of us celebrating, and I was pleased to get back to Leeds. The thought of that 12-year-old girl stayed with me for ages.

Despite dodgy times like these, I still get excited every time I get a call telling me I'm needed for a fight abroad. Most of the time I end up in places I could never have dreamed of as a kid sleeping in Dad's wagon.

EIGHT

I've Still Got the Nina Ricci Soap

Boxing is constantly under threat from people who want to see it banned. I'm sure the campaigners who condemn the sport are well meaning, but I find they are usually comfortably off, middle-class people, who think they have the right to tell the rest of the world what's good for it. They fail to grasp that for many fighters, not well-educated and without many alternatives in life, boxing provides the only way we can make anything of ourselves. These critics associate a fight with anger, but boxing is not about anger – as soon as you lose your temper in the ring, you lose. Boxing is about controlled aggression. It's also about friendship, camaraderie and doing one of the two things that come naturally to most healthy males – fighting and making love.

Reformers should understand that if they ever succeed in persuading the government to ban boxing in Britain, they won't stop fights taking place. No one is forced to go into the ring and while a few fight simply to escape poverty, the majority thoroughly enjoy it. If it were banned, a lot of fighters and officials would simply re-license in places like Holland or the Republic of Ireland. That's certainly what I would do. But most would take part in illegal shows that would spring up like bootleg bars during prohibition. Underground, uncontrolled boxing would be a very dangerous thing. The stewarding of crowds would be non-existent, gambling would take on a frightening significance, and all the good work that has gone into making the fight scene safer for those who choose to take part in it would go out of the window. Do these people really care about the boxers' welfare, or do they simply want to ban a working-class sport they don't like? I don't hear many calls to ban rugby union, where a lot of young men end up with very serious injuries and, until recently, didn't even have the benefit of making money out of it.

When I talk to the anti-boxing lobby I remind them that most boxers couldn't hold down jobs like theirs. So by what right are they trying to stop fighters following a trade that is legal, where they can earn good money and be somebody? I hear people say that a large number of fighters end up penniless. Some do, but that's their choice – they earned it and they spent it. At least they had the opportunity to be secure. The fact that they don't all make the most of that chance is up to them – and they did have the experience of having a few bob in their pocket to spend on the luxuries many of their critics take for granted. Most people never get a chance to taste the good life.

The image of boxers as thick, punch-drunk dupes, being exploited by mafia-style managers like whores by a pimp, is also wide of the mark. Sure there are managers and promoters who rip the fighters off, but there's no more exploitation in boxing than in the City or big business. Nothing in boxing matches the kind of rip-off you find in a company like Enron. And while many boxers may not have high IQs and a few may be easily led, most are pretty smart when it comes to knowing what is best for them. If boxing is just for thickies who need protecting from themselves, how do the critics account for the highly intelligent, well-educated people who choose to fight? Nicky Piper is only two points behind Margaret Thatcher in Mensa, and the Christle brothers from Ireland could hold their own with most of the protestors. All three were top amateurs and successful pros, each holding an Irish title. Terry was middleweight champion of Ireland and France, and lost only one of his 18 fights. He's now a consultant surgeon in Massachusetts. Joe is a barrister in Ireland, has a degree in theoretical physics and accountancy qualifications. Mel is the equivalent of a QC in Ireland and heads the Republic's boxing. Baby Jake Matlala, the former world light-flyweight champion, went out and got himself a bachelor of commerce degree, so he could 'look after the money I've made'. I'd also remind those who claim boxing makes you slow-witted that Bob Hope was a pro fighter under the name of Packy East before he set off on the road to Hollywood.

There are plenty of fighters, Frank Bruno and Gary Mason among them, who will tell you they were heading for a life of crime until someone got hold of them and put them in a ring. I know I wouldn't have been anything if it hadn't been for boxing. It's been the making of me. I've met kings and princes, travelled all over the world, found loyal friends and had a wonderful life, all because I started boxing as a kid. I don't think anyone has the right to prevent me, or anyone else like me, from doing that.

I thought about how much boxing had done for me, a kid brought up in foster homes and caravans, as I sat by the rooftop swimming pool of the Monte Carlo Grand Hotel, looking across at fellow guests Boris Becker, Ringo Starr and Jean Alesi. I was in town to referee the WBC cruiserweight title fight between Anaclet Wamba and Adolpho Washington, and found the promoter had put us in one of the world's most famous hotels. It's so classy it must have almost as many stars as the Milky Way. It's built on the tunnel that you see on TV during the Monaco Grand Prix. The rooms are like individual palaces, each overlooking the sea – God knows what the suites must be like. It's like something out of the posh magazines or a James Bond movie. There were phones everywhere and in the bathroom there was a selection of Nina Ricci soaps – I've still got some of them at home.

I was there with Larry O'Connell, who's a straight-up guy, a great referee and was once a bloody good fighter. We lapped it up. The night of the fight was one of those balmy Mediterranean evenings you don't often get in Leeds, so Larry and I decided to stroll along the harbour to the sports complex. We looked the part in our dinner suits, and hoped we had the right air of Fred Astaire nonchalance to give the impression we did this every night of our lives. The venue was several planets away from the kind of places I used to box in. It was all starched linen and silverware. Not much screaming and shouting here. And I have to say the fight lived up to its surroundings. It was a mandatory defence by Wamba, and there was not much love lost between the pair of them. They put up a cracking display that was a pleasure to handle – once I got used to the inter-round entertainment.

As soon as the bell sounded at the end of the first, I went to collect the judges' scorecards only to find myself surrounded by a ringful of stunning dancing girls with long legs and tiny costumes. Thirty seconds later, they'd gone. For the first couple of rounds I thought someone had slipped a mind-bending drug in my drink. But then I started to enjoy bobbing and weaving my way in and out of them to collect the cards.

The fight was nip and tuck and at the end it was declared a draw – one judge for each and Larry O'Connell scoring it even, something he was to do in more controversial circumstances a few years later at the Lennox Lewis–Evander Holyfield fight. He wasn't wrong in either case.

After the fight there was just time to go back to the hotel and soak up a bit more fantasy. But if I'm honest, as much as I enjoy dipping in and out of that kind of jet-set luxury, I wouldn't want it full time. Living like that, I think you miss out on real life. I enjoy popping down the pub for a quiz night, or standing on the touchline to watch Queens rugby league team. I'm sure if you've got the money to live in the rarefied atmosphere of the Grand, a lot of the excitement of real life passes you by. You also miss out on a lot of the characters that I love to come across, people you only find in down-to-earth places. I always smile at the memory of the Hunslet scrum-half who got fed up with always being substituted about an hour into the game, so before one match he went through the bag of numbers, took out the seven and threw it under the stand. Midway through the second half he looked across and saw the coach frantically searching for his number. His triumph, however, was short-lived because a minute later he was dragged off by the coach holding up a five and a two.

The Monte Carlo Grand was certainly the last word in luxury, but to my mind some of the other big hotels don't live up to their billing. I wasn't that impressed with the Grosvenor in Park Lane, but maybe my judgement is coloured by the fact that I had to slip out early to avoid getting a bill. Don't get me wrong, the tab was paid, but I was worried in case the receptionist stopped me and asked me for the cash on the spot. I didn't have enough on me. It came about when I was doing a judging job on the Penta Continental super-featherweight title between Jonjo Irwin and Harry Escott. The fight finished late and we were in the bar afterwards, trying to get a second mortgage to pay for an orange juice, when I found out that because the referee and other judges were from London, the promoter had overlooked booking me a room. TV commentator Gary Newbon came to my rescue, saying I could have his room because he'd got to drive back to the Midlands for an early appointment.

It was a nice enough room, though a bit old-fashioned. I certainly wouldn't have paid a lot to stay there, I'm more a Holiday Inn man. I settled down to kip when it occurred to me that while Gary is tall and stocky, I'm shorter and skinny. I started to worry that the hotel might notice the difference and get stroppy when I handed in the key the next morning. Worse still, they might demand that I settle the bill on the spot rather than sending it to ITV. As with all three-in-the-morning worries, the picture got grimmer the more I thought about it, and before long I could see the police being called in when the management discovered I had about enough money on me to pay for a blanket on the basement floor. I came up with a plan to leave the key in the room and slip out quietly to catch the half past six train back to Leeds. I took the stairs because I thought the receptionist would notice me coming out of the lift. When I reached the lobby there were three people at the desk, so I walked smartly across the foyer with a cheery 'Morning'. Once I was out of the door, I sprinted to the corner, picked up a cab and headed for the station.

I was able to return the favour to Gary when I bumped into him outside the Albert Hall before Frank Bruno's comeback fight against John Emmen, which I was refereeing. I was having a cup of coffee at the BBC catering caravan at the back of the building when I spotted him. At the time he was the biggest name in TV boxing, the man who was in the corner with his mike quicker than one of Bruno's bodies hitting the canvas, and whose questions were often tougher than their punches. But at the time he had a problem with Mickey Duff and couldn't get past the security man. 'No problem,' I said, and we gibbed him in with me.

One of the most enjoyable trips I've been on was to Trinidad, where I almost ended up playing rugby for England. I got a call one Tuesday to tell me that Larry O'Connell had been forced to pull out of a judging job in Port of Spain. Could I be at Heathrow the next day? I was still married to Rita at the time, so as you can imagine the news didn't go down too well, especially when I told her I didn't know how long I'd be away. I promised to phone as soon as I picked up my ticket but I nearly bottled it when I found my return wasn't booked for eight days.

I made sure I didn't have much change when I called home and was relieved when the pips came to my rescue before Rita could get into full flow on the other end.

Despite being trapped in my window seat by one of the largest women I've ever seen, I was asleep before the plane left the runway. I woke up somewhere across the Atlantic and called the stewardess for a drink, only to be told the bar had already been drunk dry. I'd noticed a group of big lads in the boarding lounge at Heathrow and they turned out to be a party of rugby players going on tour and taking an enormous thirst with them. They were part of the same public holiday entertainment as the fight – they were due to play in the afternoon, with the WBC light-heavyweight title clash between Canadian Donny Lalonde and local boy Leslie Stewart the highlight of the night.

My introduction to the Trinidad Hilton was confusing. Given a key for a room on the tenth floor, I pressed the button on the lift and it went down. No wonder they call it the upside-down hotel. After a quick wash and change into suitable clothing, I went to the pool, where the rugby team was already well established. Chris Ralston called me over and invited me to join them for a drink. With my sweet tooth I was soon persuaded to follow their example and have a pina colada. Chris caught the waiter's eye: 'Can I have 18 pina coladas, please,' he said, adding as the guy walked off, 'and can you bring them every ten minutes.'

It was some session, but as arranged in the enthusiasm of late-night drinking, I staggered out the next morning to join in their training. I've often thought I'd like to have been a rugby league player if I'd not gone into boxing. It's a great sport, very honest and, unlike soccer, there's no chance for people to make a living poncing around. There are no fanny merchants in rugby league and nowhere for cowards to hide. I've had a lot of pleasure being involved as fitness coach with Queens, one of the top amateur outfits in Leeds, who combine skill with a physical presence that makes them formidable opposition. Rugby league is my favourite sport outside boxing. You can have a good old tear-up with no one complaining. The only problem is that women have started to creep in there as well now. I suppose, like a lot of people from the north, I'd thought of rugby union players as being a bit stuck up – hooray Henrys who liked to throw a bread roll or two, but I enjoyed working out with the guys who certainly knew how to recover from a night of over-indulgence. My own alcohol tolerance is a lot lower but fortunately they were quite gentle with me.

Later, while I was resting in my room, the phone rang. It was Jose Sulamain, the president of the WBC, and he was clearly agitated.

'Mickey,' he said, 'you must not do it. I forbid it. You could be badly hurt and be unable to judge the fight. You must not do it!'

I didn't have a clue what he was going on about and it took a couple of minutes before I twigged that he'd been looking at the hotel notice board, where unbeknown to me, Chris Ralston had posted the team for the rugby match with me on the wing. I assured Jose there was no way I was going to play. I may be crazy, but not that crazy.

The fight went well with referee Marty Denkin stopping it in the fifth, so I was able to get back to enjoying life at the Hilton. The rugby lads were around for the rest of the week and we had a great time together, and it was a bit of an anti-climax when they moved on to play the next match of their tour in Barbados. After a couple of boring days in paradise on my own, I was ready to go home and was looking forward to getting back as I went to check out about half an hour before the airport taxi was due to pick me up. The desk presented me with a sizeable bill for three days' stay. Apparently my plane ticket was for eight days, the hotel reservation for five. The hotel threatened to keep my luggage until I settled up and it took all the smooth-talking Vann know-how to persuade the manager that the promoter had made a mistake and would pay.

I just managed to catch the plane and when Rita met me at Leeds–Bradford airport I quickly gave her the present I'd bought, hoping it would improve the atmosphere. It didn't have a chance because in exchange she gave me a letter to say I had to be in France the next day to referee the European featherweight championship between Farid Benrejeb and champion Jean Marc Renard from Belgium. From the heat of Trinidad to the heavy frost of marriage in one short letter.

The USA is my favourite destination, with Italy a close second. I choose the States partly out of professional pride because I know how tough it is to get them to accept English referees. I get a real sense of satisfaction every time I'm invited to go over there. I also love the country and the people, especially in Connecticut.

My first fight there was as a judge on 'The Homecoming' – Marlon Starling's return to Hartford to defend his WBC welterweight title against Yung Kil Chung. It was love at first sight with me when I first arrived in the States. I was knocked out by the fantastic views over the city from my room on the 26th floor, and when I put on the TV they were showing the Kevin Costner movie *Field of Dreams*, which I found inspirational, especially the storyline about Costner's character, Roy Kinsella, and his father.

The next morning I woke about half past six, full of energy despite having only had three hours' sleep, and decided to explore Hartford. It's a fantastic, lively city on the banks of the Connecticut river, and as I wandered around looking at places like the Old State House, I found myself agreeing with local hero Mark Twain when he wrote: 'Of all the beautiful towns it has been my fortune to see, this is the chief.' Feeling a bit peckish, I decided to cross the road and join the queue at the Dunkin' Donut but before I could get across, a police car drew up alongside me. A huge copper got out to find out what I was doing. I must have looked like some kind of undesirable, but as soon as I explained this was my first trip to America and why I was there, his attitude changed and he became very chatty. Like many Americans, he didn't seem to have much idea about the rest of the world – he thought I sounded like an Australian. To get my own back, I told him I was disappointed in his car. It wasn't at all like the gleaming black and whites you see in cop shows over here. This one looked about ready for the scrapyard, with dents and bumps all over the place. 'Hey, buddy,' he chortled, 'this is a working car and we've had a hard night.' He showed me the various gadgets they had on the car and when he opened the trunk there was a small arsenal in there. Before he drove off, he crossed the road, went straight to the head of the queue and brought me back a bag of donuts.

Later that day I bumped into the Hartford police again when I was out shopping for some 501s for Karen. They were all the rage in England at the time but very expensive, while in the US they were much cheaper. I knew she wanted a pair and it always made me feel good when I saw how pleased she was that I'd taken the trouble to find something she wanted. I'd been told about a particular department store that stocked them but I couldn't find it on my map. I eventually

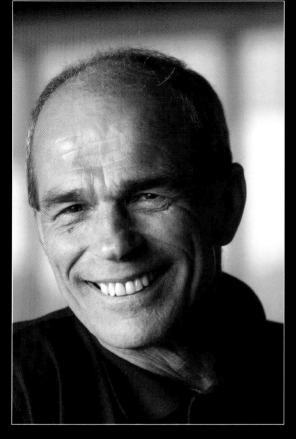

LEFT: That smile has got me into and out of plenty of scrapes in my life.
(*Yorkshire Post*)

BELOW: Dad was a big star and his knife-throwing act had them holding their breath all round the world.

Christmas Greetings
and every Good Wish
for
the New Year

from
Olga & Ralph

"The Denvers"
51, Blenheim Gardens,
Brixton,
London. S.W.2.

TOP: Always the showman, even Dad's Christmas cards promoted him and Olga

ABOVE LEFT: What a good-looking kid I was.

ABOVE RIGHT: My brother, Monty – he and I fell out a lot when we were kids.

ABOVE: That's me as the
Giraffe-necked Woman.

RIGHT: That's Dad in his
clown's outfit alongside
the car he and I used
to drive into the ring.

ABOVE: Dad and my mum, Ella, after a rehearsal. She still seems to be smiling despite the tell-tale bandage round her leg that suggests one of his chivs got too close for comfort.

LEFT: We look as though the day had gone smoothly, don't we. Check out that barnet!

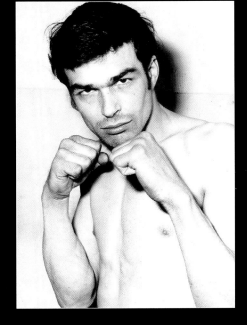

BOXING REF IN CRIME PROBE

By PETER LAZENBY

A LEEDS boxing referee has been questioned about gifts he allegedly received while acting as one of the judges in a world title fight in Texas.

The questioning is part of an investigation by a special committee of the United States Senate into links between boxing and organised crime.

The referee, Mickey Vann, is at the centre of controversy over a decision to declare a top welterweight fight a draw.

Mr Vann, who was seen by

CRIME

Mr Vann, who runs a skip hire business in Leeds, was today not at his semi-detached home in Whitehall Road.

The Senate investigation into links between boxing and organised crime has been under way for over a year.

Mr Vann has been questioned over a world title welterweight fight in Texas last month between Mexico's Julio Cesar Chavez and American title-holder Pernell

He denies claim over fight 'gifts'

Lewis world title bout a week ago, has angrily rejected allegations that he received gifts.

Mr Vann was a judge. Controversially the fight ended in a draw.

Mr Vann has been questioned over American allegations — which he denies — that he received gifts and accommodation worth $55,000 from the promoter of the Chavez Whitaker fight.

SCORED

Mr Vann has described the allegations as "a load of bullshit" and says his total hotel bill in Texas was £280.

Mr Vann has been questioned

about the way he scored the Chavez-Whitaker fight.

Today Mr Vann was adamant he had done nothing wrong.

He said the investigation into links between boxing and organised crime were not new.

"They have had allegations against me that I received gratuities and it is bullshit," he said.

Mr Vann said there were three judges at the fight in Texas, and he and one other had scored the fight a draw. The other had differed on only one round.

He also said he was receiving full backing from Britain's boxing organisations.

"They have just backed me up 100 per cent.

"I have had a bollocking about my language, but that is about all."

Tonight Mr Vann is due to referee a British title eliminator fight on the same bill as the Chris Eubank — Nigel Benn fight in Manchester.

Eubank: Page 16

▲ MICKEY VANN: Strongly denies charges

TOP: Mean, moody and not bad on occasions.

TOP: Before the storm: the officials at the notorious Chavez–Whitaker fight. L–R: Me, referee Joe Cortez, and the other judges, Jack Woodruff and Frans Marti.

ABOVE: I'm always willing to learn, so I went to pick the brains of Leeds Tykes' coach Phil Davies to help with my fitness programme for the Queens.
(*Yorkshire Post*)

TOP: You've got to be near enough to the action to see
what's going on without getting in the fighters' way.
(Paul Speak)

TOP: The greatest night of my life – the heavyweight championship of the world between Frank Bruno and Lennox Lewis at Cardiff.
(Press Association)

ABOVE: Family man: here I am with Marie and my little grandson, Benjamin. Maybe it's time to settle down!

spotted a copper on point duty in the middle of a junction and went up to him to ask for directions. He looked at me as if I was a streaker at a ball game. He stopped the cars. 'You ain't supposed to be out here,' he said. I apologised and explained that I was English and lost. 'No problem,' he laughed, then told me how to find the store and saw me to the side of the road before letting the traffic on its way once more. Dixon of Dock Green is alive and well and living in America.

The fight was a bit one-sided, but it went the distance, with Starling taking a unanimous verdict. I was just making my way to the bar when I heard an English voice call out: 'Mickey! Mickey Vann!' It was Denis, the former landlord of the Brick pub in Tong Road, Leeds, where I sometimes drank. He'd always been a fight fan but this was the first boxing he'd been to since moving to live in New York. It was just coincidence that his wife had persuaded him to take in this fight for his birthday. We had a great evening, catching up on each other's news and recalling old times. A couple of days later I had a call from his wife telling me that he'd not stopped talking about what a good time he'd had. That made my trip, and it was a bit of an anti-climax to go back home.

Not all my meetings with the American police were as happy as those in Connecticut. Things turned quite ugly when I went to Las Vegas. Nevada has been a closed shop to outside officials for years and you still don't get to referee in Vegas if you're not from the home state. So it gave me a big kick when I was called up as late substitute judge for the WBC super-welterweight championship fight between Meldrick Taylor and Terry Norris. With such short notice I had to buy my own ticket and fly in via Minneapolis. And I didn't have time to get a work permit. I filled in the white immigration form, as I'd done on my previous visit, but this time they sent me to a different queue to the one everyone else was in. I was told to take a seat and wait. Eventually I was summoned to a woman at a large desk at the end of the room. I was already feeling a bit anxious but now I knew there was a problem. It's hard enough to get a woman to listen in normal circumstances, but put them in a uniform with a gun and behind a big desk and you've got no chance.

I explained that I was only being paid my expenses and answered all her questions. She passed the buck to her superior, who told me he was putting me on the next flight back to London.

My heart sank. At last I was booked into Vegas and they were going to send me home before I'd even got out of the airport. If that happened there would be no way Don King would give me the thousand dollars for my fare. I politely told him he was making a mistake and that if he bothered to phone the Mirage Hotel and speak to Jose Sulamain, the president of the World Boxing Council, it could all be sorted out very quickly. I added: 'I'm going nowhere. I'm here to judge a world title fight and that's what I'm going to do.'

They took me to a small room with a video camera high up in the corner. I heard the snick of the lock as they went out. I took my stress ball out of my pocket and did my take of Steve McQueen in *The Great Escape* for the benefit of the camera. I figured they'd left me there to stew on things, see sense and give in. But when God dished out good sense I must have still been in the queue for stubbornness because I was determined not to be intimidated. An hour went by before a customs official came in to tell me I'd missed the first flight but there was another in two and a half hours. 'That's great, but I won't be on it,' I said.

Another hour passed before he came back in with one of his mates to tell me the flight was boarding and they were going to put me on it. By now I was pissed off. This guy was a typical jobsworth. He hadn't even bothered to phone the Mirage to check my story. 'Look, pal,' I said, 'the day a Brit rolls over and trots behind someone like you like a lapdog never existed.' When I told him that if he tried to force me on to the plane I'd thump him, he just grinned like an idiot and patted his gun. I tried to speak as calmly as I could but I could feel myself losing it: 'If you pull that out, I'll ram it up your arse where your brains are. All you've got to do is phone Jose Sulamain and we can sort this out.'

They left me to stew for another half hour then told me I had two choices – get on the plane or be arrested and go before a circuit judge. That would mean risking being deported and banned from re-entering the States for anything between a year and life. This was getting heavy and my chances of refereeing in Vegas or Madison Square Garden one day were now looking slimmer than Don King being made Pope, but it was May and the sun was shining, while back in Leeds it had been pouring down with rain. 'I'll go before the judge,' I said.

'He won't be round till the end of June,' came the reply with a smug grin.

I was determined that nothing he said would shake me now. 'That's OK. The weather's great, you'll have to feed me and find me a bed – it'll be like a six-week holiday. Can I ring my girlfriend in Leeds and tell her I won't be back for a bit?'

He'd tried all his lines now and gave up, taking me to his superior who decided to ring the Mirage. The smug look that was probably on my face then soon disappeared when the hotel said Jose Sulamain was out and wouldn't be back until the morning. It was arranged that we would ring back at 8.30 a.m. Meanwhile my passport was confiscated and I was held 'in custody' in the Holiday Inn. As ordered, I was down in the foyer by eight the next day. 'Are you getting the airport bus, sir?' the porter asked. 'Nah, there's a car coming for me,' I replied as the black and white drew up outside.

Finally the WBC persuaded them to let me in but I'd no sooner reached the Mirage Hotel than I needed Jose Sulamain's help again. They wanted a four hundred-dollar deposit against possible phone and bar bills, but I didn't have anything like that on me and didn't possess any sort of credit card, so I had to ask Jose to stick it on his card. He's got a lot of critics and I'm not the biggest fan of the WBC, but I have to say he's always treated me well and I think he's done a lot of good for boxing.

The fight was magnificent – four rounds of bedlam before Norris stopped Taylor, who was no mug, having gone within a couple of seconds of beating Julio Chavez. Afterwards I was introduced for the first time to the Nevada system of post-fight analysis, which I think should be copied all round the world. The referee and judges sit with the local boxing commission and are questioned on their performance. For example I'd marked one round differently from the other two judges and was asked to explain why. That kind of discussion is a good way for officials to learn and improve, provides the people who appoint them with an insight into the way they work, and perhaps most importantly, puts details of any controversy on the record immediately after the fight.

I returned to Connecticut as referee for the WBU heavyweight championship fight between Bobby Czyz and Corrie Sanders. I knew the officials in Hartford rated me but I feared they would think I was too small to get in among those giants, so I was chuffed when I got the call. Another Englishman, Danny Gill, was supervisor, and Charlie Payne, a former Boxing Board of Control inspector from London, was there to learn the job. My judges were William Hutt, Glen Feldman and Julie Lederman, the daughter of Harold Lederman, who with Larry Merchant is the top TV commentator on Home Box Office fights.

Danny Gill introduced me to Julie, a striking 30-year-old blonde. I was very impressed and thought it only right that I should take her under my wing. We got on really well and at the end of the meal that night, as the only smokers in the party, we went outside for a quiet cigarette. While we were chatting, I spotted Cedric Kushner, the promoter, and took Julie over to say hello. I decided to have a bit of fun and introduced her as my fiancée. Cedric, who had known her since she was a tot, didn't miss a beat and said 'My dear, how nice,' but her father was far from amused when the story reached him. He was down south for an Oscar de la Hoya fight and he spent an uncomfortable day because his colleague Larry Merchant was threatening to announce on air that Julie was about to marry a limey referee. Julie took it all in good part but trumped me with a great put-down. She waited until we were surrounded by people before saying: 'Oh, Mickey's so good – for a veteran!'

The fight was short but explosive. Corrie Sanders is a 6 ft 5 in. South African southpaw, about 17 stone, dead cool, with a faster jab than Lennox Lewis. Bobby Czyz, another boxing member of Mensa, had been out of the ring for about a year but he was a former WBC champion and looked the part. He tried everything he knew, but Sanders, who is a quick starter, never wasted a punch. He caught Czyz in the second with an awesome combination that put him down for a five count. I continued to the mandatory eight and he put his hands up when I asked him if he was OK. But I was still concerned. 'Walk towards me, Bobby,' I said, and he staggered forward like a drunk. That clinched it – I waved the fight off.

The local commissioner of boxing, John Burns, climbed into the ring saying, 'Great stoppage, Mickey,' then went over to his own officials and said: 'That's how you're supposed to do it. That's what I've been telling you in the seminars.' I thought: 'Shut up, John. They'll never invite me back.' But I have to admit I was quietly delighted when he insisted on having his photo taken with me. I was chuffed because

British referees are not always held in the highest esteem and I chalked one up for our lads – Dave Parris, Larry O'Connell and Roy Francis, all ex-fighters and our best referees.

Knock-downs are a crucial moment for a referee and it's vital to handle them right. If a fighter hits his head on the canvas or goes down hard, I stop the fight immediately, get him on his side in the recovery position and take out his gum shield, by which time the doctor is in the ring and I can step back. But other than that I count it, looking into the fighter's eyes so I can see if he is able to go on. When he gets up, I make sure I take my time, wiping his gloves on my shirt while still looking into his eyes and talking to him. There's no rush. You've got a lad's life in your hands and you have to be sure he's OK to go on. I think we sometimes stop fights a bit early these days, but that's erring on the side of safety. I remember that when I first started reffing, the BBBC secretary Ray Clarke used to bollock refs who stopped fights instead of counting someone out, because after a KO there's a compulsory medical.

Danny, Charlie and I were supposed to stay in Hartford until the Thursday but there was an enormous storm, with cars abandoned all over the place, so Cedric suggested that we stay at his place instead. He's South African by birth and has established himself up there with Don King and Bob Arum as one of the top promoters in the world. His home matched his status. A stretch limo, complete with bar and TV, picked us up at the hotel and took us to Long Island. After three different ferries, we passed through Southampton, Northampton and several other Hamptons, and at one stage slowed down so Cedric could point out what he described as the most expensive house in America – you needed binoculars to see the end of the driveway. We drove on through woodland until we arrived at the electric gates of Cedric's house. We swept up the driveway to the six-car garage with a Ferrari Testerosa, Porsche Carerra, a Merc coupe, a Chevrolet Jeep and one or two runabouts. Round the corner there was this mansion with its own tennis court, indoor and outdoor Jacuzzis, a 12-ft deep swimming pool and a gym. Cedric is obviously a bit of a TV fan because there are 48 sets in the house – I had three in my bedroom and there are five set into the wall of the living room. It was quite an experience, especially when Danny and I were sitting watching several programmes at once, only for a clap of thunder to black the whole lot out.

When we arrived Cedric told us to make ourselves at home and shot off for a meeting, so Charlie and I had a game of football on the tennis court, then cooled off in the swimming pool. It was dinnertime before our host returned, and we sat down to a superb meal that was delivered to the door. The house has a magnificent kitchen but I don't think anyone ever cooked there. Cedric was happy for us to stay there for the three days until our flight but Danny was keen to get back, so the next day we were chauffeured to the airport. The driver had started back before we discovered that our tickets were not transferable and I envisaged us hanging around an airport for two days that could have been spent in luxury at Cedric's. I was planning to get a taxi to chase after the chauffeur when Danny told me he'd paid a hundred and sixty quid out of his own pocket to change the tickets. It was back to a semi in Leeds instead of a Long Island mansion. Ah well, easy come, easy go.

Not all my travel in Connecticut has been in stretch limos. I went over to referee Miguel Angel Gonzalez, who'd had 30-odd fights unbeaten, against Marti Jacabowski with a record of only a single defeat in 82 bouts, and that at the hands of Chavez. It was for the WBC lightweight title and one of five world championship fights on the bill in the Foxwood Leisure Centre. Officials arrived from all over the world and we were met at the airport by a man mountain with hands like shovels and a face that looked as though he'd lost an argument with a baseball bat. Several of us piled into his old transit for the three-hour drive from Newark and, as I suspected with a face like that, our driver turned out to be a former fighter. Argentinean Alex Miteff was a top-ten heavyweight in the '50s and had decked Henry Cooper before losing on points when they fought in London in 1960.

We hadn't got far before smoke started to rise from under the bonnet and things started to smell decidedly dodgy, but we arrived at the Two Trees hotel in Foxwood with no mishaps. The hotel is built in stunning countryside with miles of woodlands and lakes. It's on Indian Nation land and because of separate gambling laws, has a huge casino-bingo hall that holds about ten thousand people. While we were there, Don Madjeski, one of the great organisers in boxing, arranged for us to go to a beautiful place called Mystery, which was like the Lake District in England without the rain. One of the supervisors staying with us was my pal, Mauro Betti from Italy, and he, several trainers and I used to go jogging just for the sheer joy of running through that countryside. Mauro's a smashing guy who speaks about a dozen different languages and fancies himself as a bit of a keep-fit expert. He's about 15 years younger than me so I was quietly delighted when I beat him home. Not bad for an old fella! But most of the time we just jogged out through the woods together, enjoying the views. We weren't bothered if we got lost, we'd just run on until we hit a road that would take us back to the hotel.

The fight went well. It went the distance and was a near shut-out for Gonzalez even though I took a point off him for a low blow. It was a great night of boxing and I had my first sight of Marco Antonio Barrera, who wiped out Frankie Toledo. I tipped him then to one day beat Naseem Hamed – one of the few predictions I've ever got right! We had a bit of a party after the fights before packing for our flights the next day. Alex was a bit late picking us up for the airport but assured us it wouldn't be a problem. We were chugging along when there was a loud bang. We'd got a puncture and when you saw the state of the tyre, the only surprise was that it had got us that far. The wheel had been on so long it took ages to budge the nuts, even for someone as strong as Alex. Back on the road, we urged him to put his foot down but he replied: 'I can't, the radiator's boiling.' Eventually we had to stop to let it cool down, and with no service station in sight, the only way out was to take turns peeing in a bottle to top up the water. We reached the airport and I grabbed my case and raced off just in time to catch my flight. Mauro was saved because his plane had been delayed but one of the other guys had to wait eight hours for a flight and the other official was stranded at the airport until the next day.

Alex had been a good fighter and was obviously down on his luck, struggling to make a go of his taxi business. As I flew home I couldn't help but think 'There but for the grace of God', and I wished I hadn't rushed off without giving him a tip.

NINE

A Pinch and Some Punches

The art of refereeing involves a lot more than just knowing the rules and being able to handle two guys intent on knocking ten bells out of each other. The most crucial call we have to make is when to stop a fight. Like every other ref, I've had some of my decisions questioned. In fact I was up before the disciplinary committee after my very first appointment as a star-grade ref. The bout was an international title fight between Errol Christie and one of Angelo Dundee's fighters, Sean Mannion. It went to points and Christie won by a mile. He'd been jabbing Mannion to the head all night, but I didn't feel he ever got far enough on top to warrant a stoppage. This was not a major title fight but the referee has a duty to give the boxers every chance, as long as their health is not at risk. Mannion was a born fighter – he'd had a couple of shots at the world title – and even though he was probably on his way down, he was still a tough proposition. He kept coming back all the time and I thought there was no danger of him getting stopped because Christie didn't have enough power.

This is where I think it's a hell of an advantage for a ref to have been a pro fighter. I've been on the receiving end so many times that I get a feeling when a boxer wants to pack it in. I can look in his eyes and know what he's thinking and feeling. As an ex-fighter you understand the rhythm of a fight. You realise that boxers hit a low, then drag themselves back up. For me it was always the fourth round that would be pretty rough, then I'd start up again. Another practical advantage is that it's easier for an ex-boxer to sense the way the guys are going to move round the ring, so you can stay close enough to the action to do your job without getting in their way.

For me there are two types of referee. The first knows the rules inside out and applies them as though he's reading a book. The other, and by my reckoning the better referee, also knows the rules inside out but he applies them with understanding, realising his obligations to the fans and most of all, to the boxers. There was an example of that when I took the Billy Hardy–Rick Raynor fight for the vacant Commonwealth featherweight belt at the Crowtree Leisure Centre in Sunderland. The lights went out in the middle of the fight. Strictly speaking you are supposed to send the fighters to a neutral corner until the lights come back on and if they don't, you award the fight to the boxer ahead on points. In this case I would have declared no decision because I don't think you should settle a championship in such a cavalier way. I decided to send them back to their corners so their seconds could keep them warm and let them sit down, ready to carry on once the lights were fixed. The situation was the same for both fighters and it wasn't as though one of them had a bad cut that could be worked on unfairly. To me that was using common sense, one of the qualities I look for when I'm assessing a referee for upgrading.

At the first six-monthly meeting of the referee's committee after the Christie fight, I was congratulated on being upgraded to star grade and then sent out of the room while the disciplinary committee discussed whether or not I should be downgraded for not stepping in to save Mannion from taking more punishment. The Southern Area Council had complained about me and I have to say I think it was partly a political act. They don't believe anyone living above Watford is any good. I was born in Camberwell but I found the London area officials very unhelpful and in some cases officious. For instance, on the same bill I reffed a fight between British and Commonwealth champion Mo Hussein and a Moroccan, Jose Mosqueda. I asked the inspector if Mosqueda spoke English and was told there was no problem, but when I went to the corner to warn him during the fight, it was obvious he didn't understand a word, and neither did anyone in his corner. That was the kind of thing the officials should have found out and made sure there was an interpreter in the corner. Perhaps they thought one of their own guys should have got the promotion to star grade instead of this guy from Yorkshire. But it was a good lesson for me – if you want a job doing properly, do it yourself. One of the most stand-offish and unhelpful people that night was London-based Johnny Pritchett, the former welterweight champion. I was surprised at Johnny's apparent unwillingness to help another ex-fighter, but you just never know with some people.

I got through the hearing OK but there seemed to be a shortage of championship fights for me that year. After a while, and many visits to my old home-town, I was finally accepted in London, but I have to say that the people in the Midlands and the North have always been more friendly. It was something I noticed when I first moved to Leeds 40 years ago.

The rules of boxing have evolved over the years and on the whole they work well, although I would personally do away with the standing count, when a referee gives a struggling boxer time to recover even though he's not been knocked down. If he's hurt, let him go down. When the referee intervenes it should be to stop the fight, not to get someone off the hook. Can you imagine the stink if a centre-forward beat the offside trap only for the ref to call him back to give the defence a second chance?

My main complaint about the rules is that the various organisations don't all sing from the same hymn sheet. Larry O'Connell pushed for a long time for Britain to adopt the mandatory eight-count when a fighter is knocked down that the rest of the world had used for some time, and he got backing from most of his fellow refs. It was brought in eventually but the arguments put up against it were typical of the view you hear too often in this country – that we are above learning from other countries. That's especially true in sport where you often get the feeling from officials that we are the only country in step. Not having the eight-count caused confusion and even cost fighters victory. I used to make a point of telling visiting boxers if the rule was not in use, but in all the confusion and panic of a knock-down they often forgot. I was the referee when a good American, Mike Johnson, met Pat Barrett in Oldham. Johnson had Barrett struggling in the opening round, putting him on the canvas, and for the early part of the second, when Pat produced a hammer blow that put the American on the deck. I sent Barrett to a neutral corner and went back to the count. I'd only reached four before Johnson was on his feet. If he'd stayed down for another four or five seconds, I think he'd have been OK to continue but he was still wobbling and I had to stop it. Johnson and his corner went mad and I could sympathise with them. For him it was the natural thing to get up and clear your head during the eight-count, but under the rules we were using he had to be stopped.

The other controversial area for referees can be the points decision. Wherever you go in the world, you will always find someone to disagree with a decision you've given. I'm not naïve, I know there have been some iffy verdicts down the years, but there are a few things the punters don't take into consideration when they start yelling 'fix'. When they are at a fight they are usually involved, quite correctly, in the whole entertainment. They may have had a few drinks, and during the fight may be discussing it with their mate or shouting support for one of the boxers. They are not close to the action, nor are they concentrating 100 per cent on what is going on in the ring. Only the referee has an all-round view. Even the judges, who have a prime ringside seat, see the fight from only one angle, and that can make a difference to the way they score it.

A case in point was the Andy Till–Wally Swift junior contest for the British light-middleweight crown that I took at Watford. It was the 1992 fight of the year, a blinding contest that I still keep on video. Wally was the champion and he started off brilliantly as he and Andy fought three rounds that were described in the *Boxing Yearbook* as 'among the fiercest witnessed in the British ring'. They were both very tough lads with good chins, but Wally was the better boxer and he was picking Andy off. The pattern of the fight changed, however, in the fourth round when Swift hurt his right hand. He was still throwing it but I could immediately tell the difference in power. He started to concentrate on left jabs and hooks. By the end of the 11th round there was nothing in it and I knew the final round would be decisive. They went at it hammer and tongs but I thought Andy Till just shaded the round because his punches were more powerful. As soon as the bell sounded I went over and lifted his hand, scoring the fight 118–117½. John Morris, the secretary of the BBBC, climbed into the ring to present the belt and said: 'Well done, Mickey. But I don't agree with your verdict.' I was taken aback because John wouldn't have said anything if he hadn't felt strongly about it. A few weeks later I bumped into him and he said: 'Mickey, I owe you an apology. I was talking to the press after the fight and all those on my side of the ring thought Swift had won, while those on the other side, to a man, gave it to Till.'

I thought about that when Larry O'Connell found himself being pilloried for giving the draw in the Lewis–Holyfield world championship fight. I know Larry to be completely straight and no matter what the pundits say, or what it looked like on TV, I know if Larry gave a draw, he saw a draw. What I found objectionable was the remarks that implied that because he is British, Larry should have leaned towards Lennox Lewis. Our job as officials is to be impartial. We don't care where a fighter comes from, what his colour or creed is, what his style is, whether he's the local boy or a body thrown in for another result. They should all get the same treatment and be judged on their performance in the ring on that particular night, not their reputation, or what the promoter or crowd would like to see.

There are times when it feels almost painful to give a bout against a fighter, because you know how hard he's worked and what a win would mean to him, but you have to be completely cold and go by what you see. That happened to me when I refereed Robert McCracken against Paul Welsley at the Aston Villa Leisure Centre for the British middleweight title. Paul's a journeyman from Birmingham with far more losses than wins to his record, but when he got his chance he came within a whisker of causing a massive upset. McCracken never seemed to find his usual form and at the end of the 11th round I had them all square and was looking for a winner. It was a terrific and pretty even last round, but McCracken landed a couple of great shots that just shaded it as far as I was concerned and I gave him the decision by half a point. Having often dreamed of coming out of the pack to claim a title myself, I knew how Paul was feeling, but he took the decision without complaint. Later, as I always do, I went to the dressing-room to check on the fighters. Paul was sitting on the bench with a towel over his head, the sweat still dripping off him and no doubt his mind still churning with all those hopes that were disappearing like the smoke from the cigarette he was drawing on. He looked up and gave me a half grin: 'I'm OK, Mickey, but I needed this fag.'

One of the things I'm most proud of in my career is that I've handled championship fights involving Crawford Ashley and Michael Gale (both of whom live not far from me) and have never had a murmur of complaint from their opponents. I've reffed Ashley twice, for the British title in Hull against home town boxer Tony Booth, and in defence of his European belt against Ole Klemetsen. There was a moment during the Klemetsen fight when I was in a position to do Ashley a favour. He was expected to win and he knew that while the Norwegian was dangerous in the first few rounds, he would soon fade. All Ashley had to do was keep out of the way and then go on and win it, but he got tagged and hurt early. At one stage he got caught with a blinding punch that staggered him, and shortly after he went down from a push. I could have started to count, which would have given him a few seconds to recover, but to me it was an obvious push and it would have been cheating to give Ashley an advantage. He was soon whacked right on the button and went down like a sack of spuds.

I fought at the same time as Michael Gale's dad, Brian, so I knew them both fairly well. I felt the lad had been pushed into the sport a bit and wasn't much in love with it. But I was delighted when I was given his Commonwealth title fight in Leeds Town Hall against Brent Kosolofski, and Michael seemed up for it when I went into his dressing-room to go over the rules. So did the Canadian – when I told him there was no three knock-down rule, he seemed pleased and said: 'So I can knock him down as much as I like?' I replied: 'Yes, as long as it's within the rules and I think he's OK to carry on.' It was an excellent fight for three rounds, then he started to beat Mike up and I stopped it. The sad postscript to that story is that when I was abroad some time later I bumped into Kosolofski's manager, who told me the lad had been locked up for armed robbery. He was a hell of a fighter and I thought he had a chance of making it to the top, but obviously he was too anxious to make his fortune quickly.

Another local boxer I refereed was John Doherty from Bradford. He was always a pleasure to handle, never giving a moment's bother. I was the referee for his first fight against Taffy Mills at the Astoria in Leeds. John started brightly but got caught with a big punch that ripped his eye open in the first. I stopped it because, although I could have let the fight carry on a bit longer, John was obviously not going to go the distance. I decided that the sooner he got the injury treated, the sooner he would be able to fight again. When I saw him in the dressing-room afterwards he was very upset and even talking about quitting the sport. I told him how impressed I'd been with his performance and added: 'Don't worry, John. I won my first fight and lost the next six. You've got championship potential and I'm sure you'll win your next one.' I don't know if that had any influence on him, but he went on to take the British title three times and win a Lonsdale Belt outright.

Of course, life being what it is, there are places where it is difficult for a visiting boxer to get a decision. Italy has a reputation as a place where if you don't knock the local boy down and nail him to the floor, you've got no chance. But to me the most biased place is Scotland. They don't seem to be able to get their head round the fact that their lads might lose. I refereed the eliminator for the British welterweight title in Glasgow between local boy Willie Beattie and Tony Swift, another son of Wally. When I gave Swift the verdict the crowd wanted to lynch me, yet Tony is a super boxer and won by three rounds.

One of the biggest travesties I've seen was when I was a judge in Glasgow on the WBO Inter-Continental lightweight title between home fighter Tanveer Ahmed and David Armstrong from America. The other two judges were Scottish. I gave the fight to Armstrong by four or five rounds but one of the other judges gave it to Ahmed and the other scored it even, making it a draw. The referee that night was Paul Thomas and he said afterwards it was so clearly Armstrong's fight that he couldn't understand how they had come to their decisions.

I've had so many problems in Scotland that now they've got their own parliament they will probably refuse to give me an entry visa. The most controversial fight I reffed there was for the vacant British flyweight belt between Keith Knox and Mickey Cantwell. I was really looking forward to the fight but it turned out to be a big let-down. Cantwell was the better boxer, Knox the more aggressive, but neither was getting anywhere. There was a lot of slapping, holding and mauling and I could see that I needed to get involved to try and make it a better fight for the fans. I moved in close and had a few words. In fact I got in so close that one of Knox's punches hit me. He looked more startled than I did. I just said 'Get on with it' and went back to trying to make a fight of it. Nothing changed, so I decided to try and provoke them into action and called them a couple of toss-pots. I said: 'You're arseholes. This is a British championship fight. Fucking do something.' It was close going into the final round and in the end I gave it to Cantwell by one round because while Knox had been aggressive, he was not as effective. As usual, there was a big outcry from the Scots. *Boxing News* carried letters for and against my decision.

The next thing I heard was that Knox's manager, Tommy Gilmour, had decided to report me for swearing at his fighter. Apparently Knox, who comes from Glasgow, remember, had never heard such language and was upset by it! Once again I found myself summoned to the Board. This was serious because even though the public hadn't heard the swearing, the Board might downgrade me. If that ever happens, if they ever say they don't feel I'm competent to handle top bouts because of my sometimes unconventional methods, I'll walk away from boxing. The night before the hearing I got a phone call from Mickey Cantwell telling me it would be called off because he'd refused to give evidence. Apparently Knox and Gilmour had been pestering him on the phone all night, but he said: 'Mickey, I was so wrapped up in the fight that I really can't remember if you swore or not. It certainly didn't affect me and anyway, even if I'd lost, I would have thought it was because of my boxing, not because the ref swore at me.'

Sure enough, the next day Gilmour withdrew the complaint. But that wasn't the end of the story. I wasn't given a title fight involving Paul Ingle and Billy Hardy after Gilmour had taken over as Hardy's manager because the Board didn't want to 'embarrass' me. That was upsetting, because I certainly had nothing to be embarrassed about, and I know that whatever differences I might have had with Tommy Gilmour or any other manager, I would still give a completely honest verdict in any fight I reffed or judged.

Talking to the boxers is part of being a good referee. You are there to help make the fight a good spectacle for the fans. I hate to keep saying 'break, step back'. That makes the referee more visible and is boring. So I get in close and try to sort them out while they are fighting. On the other hand, if it's been a hard contest where they've both been having a go and are starting to tire, I'll wait for a clinch and say: 'Have yourselves a few seconds, lads. You've done great. Look as though you're doing something, then break away and get back at it.'

Sometimes words are not enough to sort out a problem and you have to get more involved. That's particularly true when a fighter is bottling it, or when he's trying to get an unfair disqualification. That's when my little arm nip comes in very handy. I used it during Frank Bruno's comeback fight at the Albert Hall against John Emmen. The Dutchman was nothing more than a blown-up cruiserweight whose only claim to fame was to be light-heavyweight champion of the Netherlands. He was yet another body put in to give Frank an easy ride and it became obvious fairly early on that he didn't really want to know. Towards the end of the first round Frank whacked him, gave him a shove, and as Emmen went down, took another swing at him. I called a time out and went over to Emmen to get him up, but he had decided he was staying there. I wasn't having that. He wasn't badly hurt and the fans hadn't paid a lot of money to see him quit at the first opportunity, so as I talked to him I got my fingers under the soft part of his arms and gave him a nip. He shot up as though someone had stuck something hot and pointed up his bum. I went over to give Frank a lecture, partly to give Emmen a bit longer to recover. But it only took another couple of punches and he was down again, complaining he'd hurt his ankle. It was a disgrace.

I had to use my pinch again when I went to Marsala in Sicily for the European light-heavyweight title fight between Eddy Smulders and Andrea Magi. On the plane going over I met a very attractive Japanese girl who was guiding a group of Japanese tourists around Europe. We started chatting and were getting on famously. In fact we were hitting it off so well that I felt confident enough to say: 'What a pity I'm not staying over in Rome. I think if I were, we would sleep together.' She said: 'Yes, I think we would.' I was just cursing my luck for missing out when a thought occurred to me. 'Do you know what the Mile High Club is?' I asked. She nodded and it wasn't long before I became a member. As I changed planes in Rome, I bumped into her party again. All the Japanese guys were pointing at me and laughing. So much for the discretion of Oriental women! Maybe they knew something I didn't – I got checked out to be on the safe side.

I suppose I should have felt guilty. Not only was I being unfaithful to my wife but also to my girlfriend. But I didn't see it like that. It was just one of those things that happen, and being a male, I took advantage of the situation when it arose. It wasn't serious and didn't change my feelings about Karen at all. I reckon it can be good for a relationship for the man to stray occasionally. It makes him feel a bit guilty, so when he goes home he is extra nice to his partner. I've always found it quite easy to seduce women and I had another fling with a Scottish girl named Irene when I sensed Karen was beginning to cool a bit. We met in a supermarket and before long I was popping round to her place quite regularly. I knew it wasn't going to be forever, but for six months we had a very pleasant time.

The Smulders–Magi fight was promoted by Roberto Sabatini and Julio Spagnoli. They were the sons of two top Italian promoters who had been in fierce opposition; when the fathers died, the sons got together and had some very good fighters in their camp. This was set to be a cracking fight. Smulders was European champion and the number one contender for the world title, while local boy Magi was number three in the world and the number one European contender. Smulders hurt him early on. He gave him a couple of stiff ones and as Magi was on his way down, Smulders was in and tried to land another, but missed. I pushed the Dutchman off to a neutral corner, went back to Magi and took up the count. He was complaining: 'He hit me when I was down.' I kept counting and he jumped up, still moaning. He looked over to his corner and they obviously gave him a signal because he went back down on one knee, groaning 'He hit me' again. I could have carried on counting but the crowd had come to see a fight, not someone quitting as soon as he got hit, so I said: 'No he didn't. If you don't get up and fight I'm going to disqualify you and you'll get no money.' I added the extra encouragement of a little nip on his arm and he got up. I had another word with Smulders to give Magi time to think about it, but when I went to start the fight, he was still protesting that he couldn't go on. I tried once more, then said: 'That's it, you're disqualified.'

The crowd went berserk. They wanted to kill me. I looked for the supervisor for some backing, but he and two of the judges had already grabbed a car and gone back to the hotel, which with hindsight was good thinking. The only person on my side was the third judge, Bob Logist, who had stayed on to help. Good old Bob, we've been through some things together – he was a judge on my first refereeing assignment abroad. I was soon surrounded by armed police, who bundled Bob and me into a car and got us back to the hotel. It was around midnight and when I saw Julio he said: 'Fuck you, I'm not paying you.' I eventually found the supervisor, who was having a pretty hectic first title fight, and pointed out to him that it was exactly because of situations like this that he was supposed to get the officials' money before the fight. I eventually got paid and went to bed around half past three. Twenty minutes later there was a rap on my door. It was the police – they had decided I'd be safer at the airport. They smuggled me out of the hotel and I spent six hours in an airport lounge waiting for my flight. But there were no complaints from me because they put me in the business-class lounge with all the freebies to make sure I wasn't bothered. They were so keen to get rid of me, they whisked me on to the plane almost as soon as it landed. I was confident I had acted properly and that was borne out at the next European referees' convention when they showed the fight on the big screen and asked delegates what they would have done. The European Board backed me to a man, and I've had plenty of European title fights since. Mind you, if you look in the record books it says Magi retired in the second, so I guess someone changed the paperwork to make sure he got paid.

TEN

The Shirt Off My Back

I've always been very patriotic, but that's not the only reason I believe we have some of the best boxing referees in the world. Our system ensures you learn your trade as you go along, and only when you've had plenty of experience and proved yourself in all kinds of circumstances do you even get considered for promotion to star grade. As I've said, I think the best refs are those who have been fighters, and that's borne out when you look at our top guys. Roy Francis had a damn good career with a few fights as a pro and 200 as an amateur. He represented England for 6 years from the age of 17 and later became the national coach. He's been beaten a few times so he knows what it's like to be in the trenches. Dave Parris had around 60 fights as a pro and 96 as an amateur. He was known as the 'Tottenham Crab' because he could grab you from the other side of the ring. Larry O'Connell fought 155 bouts with 122 wins – he certainly knows what it feels like in there. Over 30 of his fights were against international opponents and he was one of the few boxers to beat Olympic gold medallist Dick McTaggart. Larry fought McTaggart three times, including the ABA final when the Scot clinched his record fifth title, but I'm not alone in thinking that Larry won that night and should have had the crown.

Of course, there are exceptions to every rule and John Coyle is certainly that. He wasn't a fighter but he is clearly one of our top officials, a fact acknowledged when he was voted the best referee in the world in 1992.

The qualification requirements for a referee aren't nearly as stringent anywhere else in the world, and without wishing to be rude about the standard of their boxing, it is difficult to see how you can get star referees from places like Austria, Luxembourg and Finland. But you do. Even American refs don't have it as tough as we do to get a licence, and that can result in officials being put in charge of bouts they aren't ready for. I remember watching one world championship bout where the guys refused to box and referee Mitch Halpin didn't have enough experience to know what to do. He had to ask Jose Sulamain at ringside. Yet he still got major fights because he came from Vegas. Halpin later committed suicide, which was sad, but to me it raised the question of whether he had the right temperament for refereeing in the first place, or just the right address.

Don't get me wrong – the Americans have some great refs, probably some of the best. But they also have many that are not as good as our best. Joe Cortez is a top referee and a nice bloke as well. Richie Steele and Rudi Battle were very good, and Arthur Mercante was just terrific. He handled 115 world title fights including the first Ali–Frazier clash in 1971, George Foreman's second-round knock-out of Frazier, and Floyd Patterson's 1960 win over Ingemar Johansson. Even though Mercante must now be over 80, he's still terrifically fit.

I suppose the American official most English fans would recognise is Mills Lane, just because he's done so many TV fights. But I have to say he's not one of my favourite people. He always gave the impression that he felt more important than the boxers and that he believed the attention should be on him. He's the kind of guy who, if he won an area title, would strut around as though he was world champion. My view of him may be coloured by our initial meeting. I was in Las Vegas for my first appointment there as a judge on one of Joe Cortez's fights. I saw Mills Lane in the Mirage Hotel and out of courtesy went over to introduce myself. The short, balding ref ignored my outstretched hand, said 'Very good' and walked past me. I was so incensed I called after him: 'You're a fucking arsehole.' I could cheerfully have decked him.

Lane is a trial judge in Reno, but his sense of justice didn't rush to the surface when he used to go on TV to comment on the ability of boxers he might one day have to referee. I was livid when I read that he'd criticised fellow referee Luis Guzman, who I know to be a good, honest and competent ref. If Lane had advice, he should have given it to Luis privately. It was no surprise to me that when he quit the ring he got his own TV show.

One of the main problems is that appointments are not always made on merit. I believe there's too much favouritism in some of the boxing organisations. I've already told you how Mike Jacobs nearly put me off my chance of becoming a star-grade referee. He was later downgraded, yet when they published a list of refs and the world championship contests they had handled, he'd had far more than some of our best refs. In five and half years as star-grade, he had 13 world title fights including Sugar Ray Leonard against Roberto Duran, Marvin Hagler's clash with Jose Camacho, and Azumah Nelson against Julio Chavez. In stark contrast, Roland Dakin had only one more championship fight in 18 years at the top, Sid Nathan had nine in nine years, and in five years John Coyle was only given three world title fights. The stench is higher than on a Hull trawler.

We are starting to break down the barriers, and I like to think the work Larry, Dave, Roy and I have done has helped. But there has still not been a non-Nevada referee in charge of a bout in Las Vegas, and we haven't had an English ref take a contest at Madison Square Garden, so there's still some way to go. I came close when I was appointed to take charge of one of Angel Manfreddy's title fights at the Garden, only to be dropped in favour of a New York referee.

There's great camaraderie among the British refs. We support each other and usually before you take a big fight, the other lads will phone and wish you well. That proved a blessing on one occasion when Roy Francis phoned John Coyle to say 'Have a good 'un' before Frank Bruno's fight against Adolpho Marin in Shepton Mallet. John replied: 'That's very nice of you, but I'm only going dancing.' The Board had forgotten to tell him he'd got an appointment. He grabbed his dinner suit and drove like mad, arriving just before the fight was due to start.

A lot of leg-pulling goes on and I love to tease the other guys. I called John Coyle once and his wife, Sonia, answered the phone. When I asked to speak to John she said: 'Who's calling?' I replied: 'The best referee in the world.' She laughed and called out 'John, it's Mickey Vann,' and when he came to the phone I said: 'See, even your wife knows who is the best referee in the world.'

On the whole we're a sociable lot and enjoy each other's company as we travel round the world together. Enza Jaccoponi, the secretary of the European Boxing Union, says it's always the Brits who make the conventions go with a swing. Certainly we seem to be the ones who are most keen to speak, with about 70 per cent of the input. The idea of these conventions is to get all the EBU officials together every couple of years, to see how we can improve the standard. We have guest speakers, analyse fights and have plenty of frank discussions, and it's always the guys from Britain who keep the whole thing going. At times it's not easy and occasionally the whole thing is a waste of time.

I remember that following a particularly good convention in Geneva, we were all looking forward to the next one in Madrid. But that only lasted until we arrived. Paul Thomas, John Coyle and I travelled out together and were a bit taken aback when the taxi took us to a building that was miles from the middle of the Spanish capital. It looked more like a prison than a five-star hotel, and turned out to be a sports centre. We were expected to stay in dormitories, with three to a room. To say the accommodation was basic would be flattering. The rooms had just three single beds, a rail to hang clothes on and a little shower compartment. There was not even a telly to while away the hours. When we had a look round the complex, there was absolutely nothing there except a small canteen-style restaurant and bar. I was already fed up and ready to go home – we might have been there for serious discussion, but you want to enjoy what spare time you've got. The others persuaded me to wait and see what Larry O'Connell, Roy Francis and John Keane thought when they arrived.

They were less than impressed but we decided to stay the night and see how things worked out the next day. We had a meal and wandered into the bar, but around five to ten the barman asked us if we wanted any more drinks because he was about to shut. When we asked what we were supposed to do for the rest of the evening, he just shrugged and said: 'Go to sleep.' That was it. We were definitely going home the next day. Roy Francis said he had a bottle of duty free in his bag, and one or two of the others had also picked some up on the way out, so we all got together in one of the rooms and got absolutely plastered. We were late getting up the next day and decided that we'd just get some more bottles and make the most of it.

The convention turned out OK and to be fair to the EBU they took us for a wonderful meal on the last night, but we weren't sorry to go home. When we arrived at Manchester airport, John, Paul and I collected our luggage and headed for customs. I went through the green channel and suddenly found myself on my own. I was still wondering where the other two had disappeared to when I reached the main concourse to be greeted by a crowd of people holding a banner that read: 'Welcome home, Mickey Vann. The best referee in the world.' I wondered what the hell was going on until I spotted Sonia laughing and twigged – I'd been stitched up. John and Paul came out and everyone fell about. For a while after that I stopped being so cocky when I was on the phone.

Adrian Morgan was one of my favourite travelling companions. He was a referee for a long time – he even reffed one of my fights, against Billy Waith in the Afon Lido Sporting club in Aberavon, giving Billy the decision. He did the job because he loved the sport and wanted to be involved. He didn't mind that it took him over 30 years to get his star grading. It's sad that he never took control of a world title fight. He could have handled it and I would gladly have given up one of mine to let him achieve his ambition. Ade was Head of Maths at a school, and in many ways a typical teacher, a bit formal and correct. But once he loosened up he was great company. Like so many of his countrymen, his passion was for singing, rugby, beer and conversation, and with his wife Joyce working as a night sister in a hospital, you always knew there was no point ringing Ade after nine o'clock in the evening; by then he'd be in the rugby club at Carleon. He played rugby for Pontypridd as a youngster and one of his mates on the circuit was Bruce McTavish, the Kiwi referee and former All Black rugby player. After one discussion on the relative merits of their country's players, they ceremoniously swapped ties – to my mind a much better way of expressing your rivalry than kicking someone's head in, like some football fans.

Ade came with me on one of my trips to Capo D'Orlando in the north of Sicily. The plane landed in the south of the island and as we walked across the tarmac we passed the chalk outline of a body. One of the security men saw me staring at it and confided that it marked a big problem – the first time the Mafia had shot a woman in 20 years. I don't know if that was just a colourful *Godfather*-style tale to titillate the tourists but it certainly made you aware of where you were.

As we went through the checks, Ade set off the metal detector and the security men became suspicious because there was nothing in his pockets likely to be responsible. I walked on and heard him shout after me: 'Mickey, for God's sake tell them I've got a metal hip joint, will you?' I laughed and called back: 'Fuck off. You never gave me a decision when you reffed me, why should I help you now?' When they eventually let him through, we were picked up by Bruno, a hulk of a man who drove us up the long coast road because, he explained, we didn't have 'permission' to take the direct route.

It was November and on the night of the fight, it was freezing. As we drove to the fight I remember saying to Bruno that I hoped the hall would be well heated. 'No problem,' he said. 'Everyone has good heating.' The venue turned out to be a huge aircraft hangar of a room and the sole heating was two packets of Victory Vs handed out to everyone as they went in. With only a thin T-shirt on under my dress shirt, I was ready to try anything but as I stood there before the fight, loyally singing the national anthem, a Victory V shot out of my mouth, looped through the air and landed at the feet of the MC. As I looked down, my Welsh judge was falling about laughing. He revelled in telling that tale when we got back, but to be fair he was also good at telling stories against himself. His favourite was when he arrived to take a fight in French Guyana. He'd suffered aggravating delays and was anxious to go to the loo by the time he reached his hotel room. Ade dropped his trousers and sat down, but before he'd even had time to settle he leapt back in the air, having felt something attack from below. His desperate getaway was halted when his trousers tangled around his ankles and sent him sprawling across the bathroom floor, bashing his head on the door. Finally, regaining his composure and his trousers, he went back to the toilet bowl where he found a black frog, looking just as startled as he was.

Adrian died on his way to boxing. He'd retired from refereeing but had stayed involved as a judge and was waiting on the slip-road to the motorway for a lift when he had a heart attack. He was dead by the time someone spotted him. All the referees were devastated. We had done so many fights together and everyone loved him. I know Larry O'Connell and Dave Parris were very upset because they were working abroad and unable to go to his funeral. Paul Thomas was the only other star-grade referee in Britain who didn't attend. The rest of us put on our dinner jackets, each with the badge of the boxing commission we worked for on the pocket, and along with one of the Welsh area referees, we were his pallbearers. There was a terrific turn-out – the church was packed with fighters, promoters and officials as well as family and friends. One thing, though, disappointed me greatly; there was no one to represent the British Board of Control in London. There should have been. But we gave him a great send-off. John Coyle made a terrific job of the tribute. I drove three of the refs back to Joyce's after the funeral and put on a Chubby Brown tape. Ade would have appreciated that.

Dave Parris and his wife Shirley were terrific friends to me and I always had a room at their house in Edmonton where I could crash when I was working in London, or going to and from Heathrow. Even when I had been stuck at one in the morning, Dave would come and fetch me and Shirley would get up and prepare something for me to eat. In recent years Shirley battled against cancer, a fight she sadly lost in August 1999. She fought hard for life even though at times she was racked with pain and the treatment was tough to take. Through it all you never saw her without a smile and she never complained. I hate women's boxing, to me it is not right, but when it came to courage, Shirley was a world champion. I saw her three days before she died and was touched to hear that a couple of days later she was still thinking about me. Dave and their son Steve were sitting next to her bed as she slept, talking about me. Shirley woke up and said: 'Dave, you're going to have to look after Mickey. Make him settle down.'

When not reffing, Dave had a flower stall, which was a major contrast to life in the ring. He and I were pro fighters at the same time so there's a bond between us, and we often have a laugh about some of the crazy things that have happened to us. One of his favourite stories is about when he and I were due to get the Shuttle through the Channel Tunnel to France. Shirley and he invited me to stay overnight, ready for an early start, and I arrived at about half past seven looking forward to Shirley's cooking and an evening in their company. As we chatted, Dave casually asked if I'd got my passport. I'd thought I wouldn't need one as we were going by train and when they assured me I did, I said: 'I won't be long,' jumped in my car and headed back to Leeds. Dave and Shirley thought it was one of my wind-ups and phoned me on my mobile to tell me to stop mucking about. It took me a couple of minutes to persuade them this was for real and to leave a key out for me so I could get back in. I arrived in Leeds around midnight feeling whacked, grabbed an hour on the bed and set off down the M1 for the second time that day. The road was clear and I was able to put my foot down, reaching Dave's place in two hours and two minutes, just three minutes longer than the train. It would have been quicker but there are speed cameras as you go through Enfield, so I had to stick to the limit.

It was Dave who came to my rescue on one of those occasions when the fans wanted to tar and feather me. In most sports the crowd become riled by decisions during the match and heap abuse on the referee. Boxing's a bit different. Unless it's a mauling, scrappy fight, the ref usually remains unnoticed until he has to declare who has won or lost. Then all hell can break out, especially if you decide against the local favourite. This particular fight was an early Frank Warren promotion at Reading for the British title between his man, Tony Collins, a travelling lad who now lives there, and Wally Swift junior. It was a stunning contest, another fight of the year, and in the end I gave it to Swift by one point. The Board upheld my decision when they reviewed the fight, but that was of no consequence on the night, when Collins' supporters decided the only 'justice' for their man was to lynch the guy who had robbed him of a Lonsdale Belt. Frank Warren, whose ending of the London stranglehold on promotions has been the salvation of British boxing, was still learning his trade in those days. He was probably struggling to make boxing pay and that night he'd not hired enough security men. Luckily for me, Dave Parris managed to bundle me into his flower van and smuggle me out. Once again I came up smelling of roses.

Thankfully security has improved greatly since then but I have to say that even if it hadn't, I would never let the crowd dictate my decision. Once you do that, you might as well pack in because the sport has lost its integrity. Of course you are aware that with matchmaking as it is, one guy is always expected to win. In fact with some of the matchmaking it would be a miracle if he didn't. But as a referee you are not there to help him win. Once you climb through the ropes both boxers are equal and are judged on what they do on the night. Occasionally a 'body' will fight above himself and produce a shock result, and the decision must reflect that. I think part of the enduring attraction of boxing is that fighters with indifferent early records, like Sugar Gibiliru and Steve Robinson, can go on and become champions.

Gibiliru had 46 contests, many of them losses, before he became British champion. I would like to see more boxers get a good background of fights behind them before being put up for title shots. People are winning championships now after fewer than a dozen fights but can't then go on to a higher level. They need more experience because the coaching is so poor these days. Too many fighters have only one way of boxing. They have no idea how to switch or do many of the basics that former fighters took for granted. The modern lads might ask what does it matter, as long as they are winning? But eventually they will come up against a top fighter and be completely out of their depth. That's why we are getting fewer world champions in Britain. It's too easy to win domestic titles because there are too many bodies being served up on a plate for them to beat.

Naturally, shock defeats don't go down well with the beaten fighter's supporters even if it's obvious that their man lost fair and square. Often they react violently, as they did when I was a judge on the Carlos DeLeon cruiserweight championship scrap with Massimilio Duran in Capo D'Orlando in Sicily. It was DeLeon's first fight since he defended his title against Johnny Nelson in Sheffield. I'd better rephrase that, because DeLeon didn't defend his title and Nelson didn't fight for it. They did something between the first bell and the last but it bore precious little relation to boxing. It was so dreadful that a joke started to circulate about a fight fan who was in hospital with a coma. They kept playing him videos of great fights of the past, like Ali–Frazier, but there wasn't a flicker from the patient. Eventually they put on Nelson and DeLeon, and he jumped up and turned off the TV!

I went to Sicily with Ray Clarke, who was supervisor for the fight. Ray was the former secretary of the BBBC, and if I'm honest I'd always thought he was a bit stiff upper lip and a boring old fart. But he turned out to be great company. The fight was sponsored by a pasta manufacturer, who handed out packets of raw spaghetti to the fans as they arrived. DeLeon was clearly the better fighter and by the end of the 11th round I had him ahead on points. But when the bell sounded to end the round, Duran dropped his hands and DeLeon stuck one on him, cutting his eye wide open. I couldn't believe it. The referee, my pal Bob Logist, had no option but to disqualify him but the crowd didn't see it that way and within seconds packets of spaghetti were flying in from every direction. Take my word for it, they hurt like hell when they hit you. I quickly ducked under the ring. I've no idea where Ray went but when I finally climbed out, he was shovelling piles of pasta out of the ring.

Ray and I also worked together in Alençon in Normandy on the European cruiserweight fight between Akim Tafer and Fernando Aiello. We booked into a cosy little hotel and went for a walk with one of the judges, Rolf Krol, a lovely fella from Germany. As we wandered around I noticed that some of the old buildings were pitted, as though something hard had bounced off them. Without thinking who I was with, I said: 'That looks like bullet holes from when the fucking Germans were here in the war.' Fortunately Rolf saw the funny side of it and accepted my stammering apologies.

The World Cup was on at the time and Ray and I watched the England games on TV in a bar. It was there Ray introduced me to calvados. I took to it instantly and was all for it when he asked our driver if we could buy some to take home. 'No problem, I'll bring some to the fight for you.' There was no sign of anything when we arrived but after the bout, which Tafer won with a KO in the seventh, the driver came over to me and told me to go over and distract two policemen who were standing about 30 ft from the door. That was easier said than done, because they didn't speak English and my French is somewhat worse than the English gendarme in *Allo, Allo*. I gave them a big smile and with suitable gestures said something like 'Blinding fight. Punch – great. Down like sack of spuds.' As I gabbled on I was looking over their shoulders watching the driver dash to and fro with arms full of bottles, which he was loading into the boot of his car. Finally I was able to say *'bon nuit'* to two very confused gendarmes. Our entrepreneurial cabbie had a dodgy still and bottling plant up the road, and had even gone to the bother of putting the calvados into lemonade bottles so there was no problem with customs. When I got back to Leeds I said to my son, Gary, 'Here, try this French lemonade, it's OK.' He looked more bemused than the French cops, but later phoned me and said it was the best soft drink he'd ever tasted.

It's not just the defeats that can cause you problems with fans. When Robert McCracken beat Andy Till for the British title in Watford, his supporters got well out of hand and wrecked the boozer next door. They also stripped the shirt off my back as I left the ring. It had been a real battle. The two fighters didn't like each other much and I had to keep getting in among them. By the end I ached all over from trying to keep them apart. I'd taken my brother-in-law, Keith, with me. He's a big guy and used to be a semi-pro rugby league prop forward and as I climbed down the steps from the ring splattered in blood, he started to come over. But his way was quickly blocked by McCracken fans who began to unbutton my shirt. Keith was ready to wade in but I stopped him because that might have started a riot, and I didn't feel I was in any physical danger. I bumped into some of those lads later in Birmingham and they told me the shirt had been framed and raised nearly £400 for charity.

I suppose the fact that someone is willing to pay that much for one of my shirts is a bit of a compliment and I have to admit that I like the fact that people recognise me and want to have a chat. It's great to walk down the street and hear someone yell out, 'Hiya, Mickey, how ya going?' There are times when I'd prefer not to talk about boxing but I always try to be friendly and have a chat. You know it's not going to last forever and it's surprising how often you get involved in really interesting conversations.

However there was one occasion when public recognition caused me some embarrassment. I always seem to lose my way when I'm driving out of London. It happened for the umpteenth time when I was heading home the morning after refereeing Naseem Hamed in his international superbantamweight defence against Juan Polo Perez in the Albert Hall. I was searching every road sign for a clue to the route to the motorway when I suddenly spotted the road I wanted. I pulled across into it and put my foot down. I was close behind an XR3 and as we approached some lights, they turned to amber. I sensed he was going through and accelerated more. He braked. The sound of bending metal and breaking glass was deafening. As we exchanged details I tried to explain that I was a stranger round there and had been trying to look for a sign to tell me I was on the right road. The words had hardly left my mouth when two blokes walked past and yelled: 'You OK, Mickey? That'll cost you a bob or two.' The driver of the XR3 was immediately suspicious. 'Here, they know you. You must come from round here, but you've given me an address in Leeds. Are you winding me up?' I explained that I'd been on TV the night before refereeing Prince Naseem to which he replied: 'Who's he?' Of all the people in London, I'd bashed into the one who hadn't heard of Nas, and it took me some time before I could convince him I wasn't trying to con him.

ELEVEN

Trying to Massage the Verdict?

Is boxing crooked? That's probably the question I'm asked more than any other. From the days of those old black-and-white movies like *The Harder They Fall* and *Someone Up There Likes Me*, the public have believed that boxing is a sport where fighters take 'dives' to satisfy the gamblers and gangsters. No doubt that has happened but I don't think it's ever been as bad as some conspiracy theorists would have you believe, and certainly 99 per cent of boxing is clean. It's one of the reasons I chose the sport. Dad wanted me to become a wrestler because I'd make more money but I knew from an early age that wrestling is just showbiz, and after years as the Giraffe-necked Woman and Iffany the Spider Woman, I was fed up with fake. If I was going to fight, I wanted it to be real, me against the other guy with the best man winning – even though it was usually the other man.

One of the main assets in keeping corruption out of boxing is the integrity of referees and judges, and I believe passionately that anyone who is appointed to those positions must have the balls to keep their independence. It's not that promoters and managers are leaving large brown envelopes of cash in your dressing-room. In fact, as some of the stories I'll relate show, it's not always possible to tell if they are attempting to 'bribe' you or if you are just being treated with old-time courtesy. I always assume the latter while making a mental note not to let it become the former.

Some people don't even spend money in dropping the hint about which fighter is expected to come out on top. Leading announcer Nat Basso also managed a few boxers, and as he got out of the ring after announcing the fight he'd just say: 'He's one of mine, Mickey.' Promoter and manager Mickey Duff would come over and greet me like a long-lost pal and tell me what a great kid he had and how he was going to go on and become a champion. I'd just smile and say, 'That's great, Mickey,' then go over and have a chat with the other corner to make sure there was no suggestion of favouritism. I don't see any harm in what they do. It's good management to do your best for your fighters and yourself, and any referee that is influenced by it should never have been given a licence in the first place. Most of the time you just get hints and favours that are probably meant to make you kindly disposed towards one fighter over another. You can never be sure, and if you said anything your host would be 'shocked' at the suggestion, so you just have to play along and make certain in your own mind that you are not influenced.

On my first trip to Sardinia I was picked up at my hotel to go for a meal with the promoter. I was on my own in the car with this big fella driving. He turned off the main road and went for four or five miles out into the countryside, far from anywhere. It was getting dark and any nerves I had weren't eased when we came through a tree-lined road and emerged in a clearing. The first thing I saw was a group of handy looking guys holding rifles. The house behind them was like a large chateau and when I went in, there was a long table with a huge family around it, women and children, husbands and brothers, and the elderly head of the house at the end of the table. I was introduced to everyone and spent three hours having a wonderful meal. It was probably all very kind and innocent, but I did wonder as I was being driven back if it was intended to remind me what an important family I was dealing with.

On one trip to Tokyo, I was lavished with so many gifts I made sure I told the supervisor so there couldn't be any comeback. I was there to referee the strawweight title between Japan's Hideyuki Ohashi and Napa Katwanchai from Thailand. Adrian Morgan was one of my judges with Barbara Perez and Rudi Jordan. I was tired after the trip but the driver who met us from the airport, who'd been looking after Michael Jackson the week before, told us he'd pick us up within 15 minutes to take us for a meal with the promoter. I had just enough time to splash some water over my face and brush my hair, but didn't bother to

change my socks, which turned out to be a big mistake. When we
arrived at this swish restaurant we had to take our shoes off before we
sat cross-legged at a low table. I just hoped no one picked up that the
iffy socks were mine. We were presented with 140,000 yen in
spending money and some beautiful hand-painted china. The waiter
brought a menu with about 20 items on it and I started to say what I
would have when the promoter said: 'No, Mickey, you eat everything.'
It was a superb meal, accompanied by saki, the famous Japanese rice
wine, which I'd not tasted before. I found it to my liking and never said
no as they kept topping up my glass. Finally it was time to go and I
discovered I was completely pissed. On top of that my legs were numb
from sitting cross-legged and it was a miracle that I managed to stagger
out to the car without dropping my china gift.

The next day we were taken sightseeing. I said I wanted to buy a
present for Karen so we were guided to a market in a long street that
led up to a temple. It soon became embarrassing because as soon as I
admired anything, the promoter's wife would buy it for me. In the end
I had to buy a bag to put all the gifts in. There was only one safe way
out – walk straight ahead and keep your eyes on the temple, though I
was a bit concerned she might spot where I was looking and buy me
that as well. Their generosity knew no bounds. When they found out
my finances didn't stretch to taking Karen to the next convention in
Barcelona, another envelope arrived with 100,000 yen and a wish that
we both have a good time. As I said, I kept the supervisor informed of
all this, but I was quite relieved that the fight, a superb contest won by
Ohashi on points after decking Katwanchai in the second, went off
without any controversy.

The only time I'm certain I was offered a bribe was in Bangkok. I was
in Ayuthaya to do the world flyweight championship between two
local fighters, Muangchai Kitakasem and Sot Chitalada. As always in
the Far East, big money was being gambled on the result.

While in Japan I'd had a massage at the Hilton hotel. An old girl
pummelled and punched me but left me feeling really refreshed and
full of energy. So when our driver, Po Jay, picked me up after a 13-hour
flight to Bangkok and offered me a massage, I said: 'That would be
great.' Little did I know. We turned up a back alley and into a brightly
lit courtyard with heavies just hanging around trying to look menacing

and not making a bad job of it. The place itself was a bit like a hotel. As you went in the front door there was a bar on one side and on the other, an area like a dance floor, only it was carpeted. In fact the carpet continued up over a bench that ran right round the room, and on up the wall until it reached the windows. I didn't notice much more about the decoration because I was distracted by the sight of about 50 of the most beautiful young women you've seen in your life.

Po Jay and I sat down to have a drink and were quickly joined by two of the girls, who sat either side of me. 'I'll leave you with these two ladies and come back for you in a couple of hours,' Po said, draining his glass. The massage in Tokyo had only lasted about 20 minutes, but what the hell. The girls led me upstairs and down a corridor to an L-shaped counter. Two more beautiful women in nurses' uniforms were there to greet us and hand over some towels. We went into a tastefully decorated room, the girls put the TV on and started to run a Jacuzzi. I won't bore you with the details, suffice to say that by the time Po picked me up I was knackered – and very relaxed.

When I reached the hotel I met the referee, Chuck Hassett from America, and the other two judges who came from Korea and Japan. We had a meal and sat around talking into the night. Eventually one of them went off to bed and as he reached the door, a girl from a table in the corner got up and joined him. The same thing happened when the Korean guy left. By now I'd twigged what was happening. It was after midnight and I needed some sleep but I knew I couldn't cope with any more 'massaging', so I sat there until nearly five in the morning. So did the girls. Eventually I headed for the lift. I'd just got in and the porter had pressed the button for my floor when one of the girls slipped in and stood beside me. She was very gracious when I explained the situation and curled up and slept beside me. I guess she had to stay on the job, so to speak.

At the weigh-in next day, Chitalada had problems making the eight-stone limit. He had become the champion when he took the title off Charlie Magri with a fourth-round retirement at Muswell Hill in 1985. But now he was getting towards the end of his career. Although he was only three ounces over, which should have been easy to lose, he had to work really hard and came back to the scales three times before he made the weight. He was clearly struggling, but fighters over there know they have to work hard to make it. It's instilled in them by the way they are treated. A top manager like Sam Pop has a lot of fighters and when you visit his luxury home, you see huge barrack-like corrugated huts at the bottom of his vast estate where the fighters live until they can make something of themselves and afford a few home comforts of their own.

That afternoon I followed my usual pre-fight routine of lying on the bed watching a bit of TV and dozing so I'm fresh for the evening. As I lay there, I was distracted by two guys talking in the room next door, where the Korean judge was staying. They gabbled on for about half an hour and while I couldn't understand a word they were saying, it stopped me going to sleep. What happened next ensured I was wide awake.

The door in the next room opened and shut and there was a knock on mine. When I opened it a guy introduced himself as a Korean promoter and asked if he could have a word with me. As soon as the door was closed he said: 'Chitalada is a great fighter but he is very old and coming to the end of his reign. Kitakasem is the future and we hope he will win because we will promote him in Korea. If any of the rounds are close and you cannot make up your mind, we have ten thousand US dollars which we would like to make as a present to you, if you will give it to Kitakasem.'

I was gobsmacked. At first I thought I might have misunderstood but no, this was clearly the offer of a bribe. I have to say that at that stage of my life – or indeed most stages of my life – ten grand would have been very useful, but it never crossed my mind to take it. I can't remember the exact words I used, but I asked him if he completely understood English and when he confirmed that he did, I said something like: 'I'm British and we are a very straight people. If you don't get out of that door, I'm going to shake hands with your fucking Adam's apple.' He never even got flustered. He just said: 'I'm sorry you feel that way, it would have been good for boxing in Korea' and left. I was really pissed off. I was angry because it had happened. I was angry that they thought I might have taken it. I was angry because part of my brain was thinking about what I could have done with ten thousand bucks.

The irony of the situation is that poor old Chitalada didn't have a chance anyway. There were about 23 fights on the bill, 22 of them kick boxing. When we got into the ring to take a bow, my feet must have sunk a couple of inches into the canvas. They'd put that many safety mats underneath that my calves were aching just standing there. An ageing boxer who had struggled to make the weight didn't have a prayer. The fight only went six rounds. Kitakasem murdered him and I gave him every round.

There were rumours around the hotel that the Korean judge had taken a bribe. I never heard what happened to him. I do know they couldn't have found enough cash for the bribe that I would accept. What price can you put on risking a career that has given me so much and means so much to me? You only have to look at the reports into the death of South African cricketer Hansie Cronje to realise that the public never forget. He'd been an outstanding player but all the talk was of his corruption. If I'd taken that money, I couldn't have faced the rest of my life having to look in the mirror every morning, and having people point me out in the street as 'the bent bastard who took cash to fix a fight'. Above all, I'd never have been able to go in the ring again. I'd never have refereed the world heavyweight championship, which was probably the best day of my life. I've done my fair share of ducking and diving, but not where boxing is concerned. This was a whole different ball game, and I didn't want to play. It's interesting to reflect that at least one other referee I know of has been offered a bribe over there, and it makes you wonder how much truth there was in the rumours of fixes that grew up around South Korea reaching the semi-finals of the 2002 World Cup.

As I say, that was the only time I've been offered money to rig a fight and as far as I know, this is the first time it's been made public. But there are still a lot of people in the States who think I'm quite a wealthy fella after taking a back-hander from Don King. The first I heard of it was after I'd got home and Karen rang me to say: 'If you haven't seen the Evening Post tonight, you'd better go and get a copy. You're on the front page.'

TWELVE

The Cheque is Still in the Post

I went straight to my local newsagent and sure enough, right across the top of the paper, next to a very iffy photograph of me, was the headline: 'Boxing ref in crime probe' and a story that I was being accused of being in a fight-fix scandal after taking gifts from Don King.

The fight in question was the King-promoted WBC welterweight fight between defending champion Pernell Whitaker from America and Mexico's Julio Cesar Chavez held in San Antonio, Texas. It was a political hot potato from the day it was announced, and finished up with the WBC feeling it necessary to publish a 24-page report to answer all the controversy that blew up around the fight. It was an extraordinary document in which WBC president, Jose Sulamain, Mexican-born of Lebanese parents, decided he needed to spell out what a good American he is. He included details of how many of his relatives had served in the American armed forces, and the number of awards he'd received from American organisations. It was set off by a page of photographs of him with King Juan Carlos of Spain, President Ronald Reagan, the King of Thailand, and Javier Perez de Cuellar, the secretary-general of the United Nations. Sulamain, who had been accused of being too close to Chavez and his manager Don King, pulled no punches proclaiming: 'I have been in the past, and continue to be, the target of so much slander, defamation, misrepresentation and vicious persecution mainly by some US Eastern Press, echoing vested interests, that I find it difficult to explain other than as racial and national prejudice, in a probable orchestrated campaign.'

Sulamain attacked promoter Bob Arum, whom he described as a

friend who 'later became my mortal enemy for no reason that I know'. He also criticised Whitaker's management team. But he saved his most vitriolic words for the Home Box Office commentator and journalist Larry Merchant, comparing him to Mexican fable 'The Midget in the Attic'. He claimed: 'Larry Merchant is a man whose attic is the microphone and newspaper column, behind which he becomes a powerful weapon used against all those he doesn't like, and those who do not fall within his controlled world.'

The fireworks started with the appointment of the officials. According to the WBC report, Whitaker's camp had gone to a great deal of trouble to exclude Mexican and Hispanic judges, and they got their way. Against the wishes of the WBC, whose neutrality clause would mean no American officials should be appointed, the Texas Boxing Commission insisted that the referee was Joe Cortez, and that Jack Woodruff was appointed as a judge, along with me and Franz Marti from Switzerland. Cortez is an excellent referee but Woodruff, a private eye from Dallas, was a big surprise. Not only had he not been involved with the WBC before, he'd only judged two world title fights in his life.

Even on the day of the fight it was clear the WBC were jittery, because Jose Sulamain summoned all the officials into a room and explained that there had been so much haggling over our appointment, we must make sure we were neutral. That pissed me off because I have always been straight and impartial, and I didn't need reminding. But I held my tongue and when he asked us who we fancied as the probable winner, I replied: 'I've no leanings either way.'

It was a wonderful fight. The Alamodrome was packed with 63,000 fans, the biggest indoor crowd for a boxing match. They produced over twelve million dollars without the millions more that poured in from pay-per-view TV. Pernell 'Sweatpea' Whitaker had suffered only one defeat. He was a classy, quick-handed boxer, the 1984 Olympic gold medallist, who had beaten Azumah Nelson and held the IBF, WBC and WBA versions of the title. He was a showman, sometimes spinning round to hit his opponent, and once pulling a rival's trunks down around his knees. He was also a hell of a boxer.

Chavez was a massive local hero with an incredible record of 87 straight wins, most of them by knock-out. He was an immensely powerful man, who had beaten Meldrick Taylor into submission, stopping him with two seconds of the fight to go. When he beat Hector Camecho the defeated man admitted: 'I couldn't keep him off me. This is the first time I've fought a man with this much courage. The pressure he put on me was amazing.' Coming out of poverty in Mexico, Chavez was bone hard. His countrymen worshipped him. On one night in Mexico City 132,274 of them turned out to watch him, surpassing the record 120,000 crowd who had crammed in to see Gene Tunney and Jack Dempsey in 1927. Chavez held world titles at lightweight, super-lightweight and superfeatherweight.

This monumental clash – one of the greatest contests in the history of the sport – was to decide which of these two incredible men deserved the title of the greatest pound for pound fighter in the world. The atmosphere was red hot, the noise deafening. The boxing was some of the best I've ever seen and when the scorecards were totted up Franz Marti and I scored it 115–115, while Woodruff gave it to Whitaker 115–113. A majority draw meant Whitaker retained his title and Chavez was still unbeaten. But it appeared that no one was satisfied with the verdict. Both fighters claimed victory. There were, however, a number of people who felt they would make a lot of money out of a rematch.

The American press were disgusted – the front cover of *Boxing Illustrated* read: 'Don't buy this magazine if you think the fight was a draw!' Most American journalists were convinced Whitaker had won comfortably and when it was discovered that I was the only judge to give Chavez the sixth round, I became public enemy number one.

The scorecards for the fight have been analysed a million ways since, but the facts are clear – in five rounds, all three judges scored it the same; six rounds were scored the same by two judges; only the last round was scored differently by all three. What is interesting about that is the fact that even Chavez's sternest critics feel the 12th was his best round and if Jack Woodruff had given it to him rather than to Whitaker, his score would also have ended up as a draw, 114–114.

The American journalists were up in arms about my scoring of the sixth round, which I gave to Chavez, while the other two scored it for Whitaker. I'm perfectly happy to admit that Whitaker probably had the better of it, but in my book he didn't win the round because he gained an unfair advantage by a series of fouls. On at least two occasions he caught Chavez with a low blow that made my eyes water, let alone the Mexican's. Joe Cortez called a time-out to allow Chavez to recover, which you only do if someone has been hurt by a foul. If I had been refereeing I would have also deducted a point, but Joe decided against that. Some critics claim that I deducted a point anyway, but that is simply not true. Only a referee can deduct a point and it shows in a separate column of the scorecard. I gave the round to Chavez because I don't believe a fighter can win a round if he reduces his opponent's ability by landing a foul blow. Once you allow that, you are opening up a path that would lead to chaos and down which boxing should not go. If you could win rounds by slowing down your opponent with an uppercut to the balls, I would never have lost a fight.

And make no mistake – that low blow did impair Chavez's ability to fight. Bob Mee started his report in *Boxing Illustrated*: 'Let's have no messing about here: Pernell Whitaker was robbed against Julio Chavez, who stretched his astonishing unbeaten run to 88 fights with the help of an undeserved draw at the end of 12 gruelling, draining rounds.' Later in the report he conceded: 'The low punch did seem to take something out of Chavez, for on my card at least, Whitaker took the next three rounds on a roll.'

The furore started almost immediately, fuelled by the fact that James Leija and Azumah Nelson had also fought a contentious draw on the same bill. The next morning some guy from the Senate committee investigating boxing came to my room and started to ask questions about how long I'd known Don King, and what our relationship was. And as soon as I got home, the phone started to ring from American TV and radio stations asking me questions. A journalist from the *Washington Post* got right up my nose. I answered all his questions and he was as friendly as can be. He asked me what I did for a living and I told him about the skip-hire business, but in his article he portrayed me as a 'refuse collector' and slagged me off mercilessly. However not every American disagreed with my verdict. I got a lot of solid support from a number of US officials, and I remember one newspaper article in which Californian referee Chuck Hassett wrote that he believed my decision and scoring were spot on.

The Senate committee got in touch again and wanted me to go to the States to give evidence. I told them I couldn't afford to just abandon my business to go to America on an issue I knew nothing about. After checking that he was indeed a senator and not another tricky journalist, I agreed to make a statement over the phone. Once again they concentrated on my relationship with Don King.

Even now there are people in the States who think of me as that limey ref who took twenty grand to fix the Whitaker fight. If anyone mentions it to me when I'm over there, I just make a joke of it saying: 'Yeah, but your postal service is so crap, the envelope still hasn't arrived.' The irony is that far from paying me twenty thousand dollars to give the fight to Chavez, Don King short-changed me. We were due to be paid a fight fee plus fifty dollars for every quarter of a million the fight was worth. That should have worked out at about four thousand dollars, but I only got half of that – two hundred in cash, the rest in a cheque. Jose Sulamain had left but when I complained to the WBC secretary that I'd been screwed, he said: 'No, that's the right money.' But it wasn't, it was just a case of King deciding 'you get what I say you get'.

The more I think about the whole episode, the more I think the whole thing is laughable. Who could believe that Don King, a man who has been down more than his share of mean streets, would pay me to make the fight a draw? As King himself wrote in an article: 'It's ludicrous. People say that Don King and Jose Sulamain fixed the judges. But if you were going to fix the judges, why would you fix the judges to have a draw? You'd go for a win. If you're going to get caught, you might as well get caught winning!'

I think the Whitaker camp were just pissed off that after all their wheeling and dealing to eliminate Mexican and Hispanic officials, and making sure the two neutral judges were people they thought would lean towards their man's boxing ability rather than Chavez's more rugged approach, they copped for a couple of honest judges.

When you think of the millions of dollars boxing generates – Don King gave over a quarter of a million dollars to San Antonio charities in the build-up to the fight – the money refs get paid is appalling. But we don't do it for the cash, we do it for the love of the sport. Anyway, I couldn't have done such a bad job, because a couple of weeks later I was refereeing the heavyweight championship of the world, the biggest night of my life.

THIRTEEN

Don't Fuck with Me!

Billed as the 'Battle of Britain', the clash between Frank Bruno and Lennox Lewis was the first all-British contest for the world heavyweight crown, so there was a lot of competition between our top refs to take charge. I thought Larry O'Connell would probably get the nod because he was more experienced than me. On top of that, there were a number of people trying to stop me getting the job. With the Whitaker–Chavez controversy still very much alive, there were plenty of jibes about letting 'that bent bastard' take the fight.

The main objection came from Bruno's manager, Mickey Duff. He said I was still under too much pressure from the accusations that were flying around, and anyway at 5 ft 8 in. I was too small to be able to get in among 35 stone of hostility. I was not concerned on either count. Pressure has never bothered me. In fact, I thrive on it. And I knew there would be no problem over my size. Boxers are dedicated people with self-discipline. It's not like football, where players behave like a bunch of spoiled kids. I've become sickened over the years as footballers try to con officials with diving and other forms of cheating, and if the referee talks to them, they feel they have the right to bawl back or ignore him. Boxers recognise I'm not in there to fight them. I'm not the enemy, I'm there to make sure that both of them stick to the rules and to protect them, and because of that they don't give me too many problems.

Apparently the WBC agreed with me and it's difficult to describe the thrill I felt when I took the phone call to tell me to keep the second of October free because I'd got the fight. It was a mixture of pride, excitement and above all satisfaction that after years of trying to become the best, I was the man chosen to take charge of the biggest fight in British boxing history. Of course the sniping didn't stop – Barry McGuigan jumped on the bandwagon, saying I should be relieved of the responsibility – but to their credit the boxers didn't object. For me, the most significant and pleasing thing was that Lewis's co-manager, Dan Duva, did not protest. He is the son of Lou Duva, one of Pernell Whitaker's co-trainers, and if anyone was going to say anything I thought it would be him. Jose Sulamain made a terrific gesture by phoning to congratulate me and say he thought I'd done a professional job in San Antonio.

The public's interest in this fight, fuelled by enormous media coverage, was massive from the day the fight was announced and grew day by day in the build-up. Bruno was the people's champion, the large loveable lad who the British public had supported from the moment he came on the scene. They adored him. On the other hand, many of them were suspicious of Lewis, the Londoner who had been brought up in Canada and won an Olympic gold medal boxing for them. He was the champion and they recognised his qualities as a fighter, but they didn't warm to him.

I didn't expect much attention until the fight itself but the people of Leeds were obviously chuffed that one of their adopted sons was going to referee this prestigious fight. A local company, Anchor Car Hire, sponsored me with a white, top-of-the-range Sierra and for two weeks I drove around like a pimp! Karen and I went everywhere in it, although I paid a price later when she went off with one of the hire-firm's managers. But right then, I was on top of the world, loving all the attention. There were big articles about me in *The Sun* and *Daily Star*, and everywhere I went people were wishing me good luck.

I went down to Cardiff a couple of days before the fight and was already starting to feel concerned about the amount of 'needle' building up between the two fighters. I knew they were both smashing fellas and at first I thought it was just the usual pre-fight animosity that you always get – it helps to sell tickets and also psyches up the boxers – but this was getting beyond that, mainly I think fuelled by Lewis's trainer, Pepe Correa. He was way out of order, throwing underwear at Frank and taunting him with remarks like 'You're going to eat your feet' and 'I'm going to take a pillow to ringside for you'. Lennox was obviously out to goad his opponent but went too far when he accused Frank of being an 'uncle Tom'. Frank was uptight and uncharacteristically rude to the American press because he thought they were being unfair to him. He was obsessed by Lennox's Canadian roots, calling him a carpetbagger and saying at one point: 'You don't have to be Ironside to know that the man doesn't live in this country – he's taking the Mickey out of the country.' He never missed a chance to play up his own London upbringing and make comments about being the only True Brit. As I attended the press conferences and other get-togethers, I realised there was genuine mutual dislike between the two heavyweights and made my plans accordingly.

You can never plan exactly what you are going to do during a fight, but you prepare by working out what is likely to happen and how you will handle it. For instance, I knew Frank was poor at fighting inside and liked to bang people on the back of the head. That could have provoked Lennox into doing something stupid, spoiling a fight that everyone was looking forward to, so I made up my mind to let them know early on that I wouldn't tolerate any funny business.

It had always been a gamble to stage a fight in an outside arena in Britain in October, and sure enough everyone started to get anxious as the rain continued to pour down in the last few days leading up to the big event. The championship contest was due to start in the early hours of Saturday morning to fit in with American TV schedules but I was at the stadium at half past eight on Friday morning to do a Sky TV interview. It was the first time I'd been to Cardiff Arms Park. I'd watched rugby from there on television many times but the reality was awesome and the ring, with its canopy, looked tiny in this vast arena. Before the interview I took a few minutes to just wander around and take in the feel of the place. Even at that time of the morning, with only a handful of people there, it still had a special atmosphere. I stood there and replayed in my mind that wonderful Gareth Edwards' try where he finished off a thrilling, pitch-length score for the Barbarians against the All Blacks, which has been tagged rugby's greatest try. Standing there beside the pitch, you got a real sense of how magnificent that achievement had been and I thought, 'Blimey, he must have been knackered by the time he reached the line'. Then it occurred to me that if I was thinking about Gareth Edwards and not Bruno and Lewis, I must be feeling relaxed about the fight.

Sky TV were clearly not feeling as laid-back and their interview concentrated on what would happen if the rain continued and affected the fight. I explained to the viewers that there were contingency plans to move the fight back 24 hours, but if the fight did get underway and was then stopped by rain in the first three rounds, it would be a no contest. After that it would go to the scorecards, so it could be important for the fighters to get off to a good start.

I went back to the hotel and got into my normal routine, watching a bit of TV and napping. I had to get to the stadium earlier than I would normally have done because in their wisdom the BBBC had appointed me to take an eliminator for the British title between Ross Hale and Carlos Chase directly before the Lewis–Bruno clash. I couldn't believe they'd done that – talk about saving a few bob on expenses! It was still raining and the wet canvas made it difficult for the lads. Both touched down several times after slipping and at the back of my mind I was wondering how it would affect the big fight. To be honest, I can't remember much about the fight but luckily there wasn't too much to concern me. Hale was well on top and Chase's corner pulled him out at the end of the eighth round.

I went back to my dressing-room and took a shower, donned the green WBC shirt, put on a clean pair of Union Jack socks, and splashed on some aftershave. I checked my pocket for the little silk flower Adrian's wife, Joyce, gave me for luck. I think it did its job and I still carry it in my wallet. My brother-in-law Keith says I'll never lose it because I've not opened my wallet since. I was ready. I made my way to the boxer's rooms to give them their instructions. It's always best to spell out things in the relative quiet of the dressing-room with the managers and seconds there. Once you are in the ring, they don't take in anything you say.

Lennox's dressing-room was rather quiet apart from Pepe Correa who, when it comes to understanding about fight preparation, doesn't know his arse from his elbow. Lennox seemed very tense, which I thought was mainly due to the cold night air, but I had expected him to be more relaxed. I went over the pre-fight instructions with him and asked if he understood. He nodded. As always, he was very polite. I checked his tapes, shook hands and wished him luck.

Then I fought my way down the corridor through cordons of Cardiff police to check on Frank. His room was much more relaxed and cheerful with a positive, confident air. All round the room there were Union Jacks and there was music playing. He turned it off when I came in and listened intently to my instructions. Again I checked his tapes. I like the tape to finish on top of the glove to stop it coming loose if there is a lot of clinching. I wanted the fight to flow and not be interrupted by a constant need for the contestants to go back to the corner to fix flapping tapes. I wished Frank well, walked out into the cold night and thought: it's shit or bust now.

Sky did another interview, asking if I was starting to feel the pressure, but I was able to honestly say that I wasn't: 'Not being able to pay your poll tax is pressure, this is fun,' I said, and I meant it. Of course I was nervous – I wanted to do a good job. But my nerves left me as I made my way to the ring. There was a pathway between two lines of police, some of the biggest coppers I'd ever seen in my life. It occurred to me that to qualify to join the force in Cardiff you must have to be 19 stone, and at least 6 ft 4 in. tall. There was one lad there who looked bigger than either Lewis or Bruno and as I reached him he took out his notebook. I thought he was going to do me for some traffic offence but he just thrust it into my hand and asked for my autograph.

Two of my judges were Americans – Tony Castellano and Jerry Roth. But I was most pleased that the third judge was my old mate Adrian Morgan. All three judges were wearing overcoats against the cold night and Tony put on a hat and scarf as well. No one could have been prouder than Ade to be at the ringside that night and I swear he grew two inches taller when opera singer Jason Howells sang the Welsh national anthem accompanied by most of the 30,000 fans packed into the Arms Park. Looking back, that is the moment that stands out most vividly from the night. I felt very content and very proud, and hoped my dad was watching at home.

The chatter of anticipation was halted by the strains of 'Land of Hope and Glory' roaring out from the speakers. The spotlight picked out Bruno and his entourage making their way through the crowd and as each section of the stadium caught a glimpse of him, the roar grew in intensity. He entered the ring wrapped in a Union Jack with the legend 'True Brit' emblazoned on his trunks. Lewis also got a warm welcome but there was no doubt who the majority of fans wanted to win. Both boxers were wrapped in blankets to keep them warm during the preliminaries, the climax of which was a massive firework display with a set-piece featuring the contestants and the fight's 'Battle of Britain' slogan blazing against the black Cardiff sky.

The hairs on the back of my neck were standing up but my mind was as cool as the Cardiff air and I remembered to touch my ear, the signal I'd arranged with Karen to let her know I was thinking about her. I felt confident I could cope with anything that came up. I didn't have to wait long to find out. The problems started even before the first bell rang. Master of ceremonies Mike Goodall stuck the microphone in front of me to say my few words which, as always, ended with, 'Good luck to both of you. Now touch gloves and come out when you hear the bell.' Correa tried to pull Lewis to his corner without touching gloves but I shouted, 'Oi, come here! Pepe, don't start mucking about. The rules state you shake hands, go back to your corners and come out at the bell. This ain't a street brawl, so if you don't shake hands, there won't be a fight.' And I meant it. I was willing to delay the start until they touched gloves. I knew that if I didn't get a grip of this one from the start, I was going to get stuffed, and I was determined that wasn't going to happen. I wanted to make this as great a heavyweight championship as it was in my power to.

Bruno started the fight well and was soon on top. Lewis was stiff and cold, physically and mentally, and couldn't find any early rhythm. I was pleasantly surprised there were no problems in the first round but I was still on my toes. I knew it would take only one incident for it to take off and I was determined to nip it in the bud as soon as it happened. Unlike soccer, these guys only need telling once. There was a clinch in the second and as soon as they went together I thought, 'This is it. Get in close before anything starts.' The thought had hardly registered before Frank clubbed Lennox on the back of the head. He'd done it so often before in fights, I was ready. I jumped in, stopped the fight, signalled a time-out and called them together. I was determined to let them know they couldn't get away with any nonsense. 'Come here!' I snapped. 'Now don't fuck with me. Don't act like a couple of tarts. This is the heavyweight championship of the world so do the job you're paid to do and don't piss me about any more.' Little did I know that my private warning, pro to pro, was being picked up by the microphones sited in the canopy and transmitted to TV viewers around the world. But I knew these guys had built up such an animosity, that saying something like 'Stop hitting him on the back of the head' or 'Behave yourselves' would have no effect. I wanted them to be in no doubts that I wouldn't take shit from either of them, and I wanted to put in their minds the thought that 'If I'm not careful that mean bastard's liable to do anything, including throwing me out'. It worked – I didn't have to step in again until the seventh round.

The first six had been mainly Bruno. He'd caught Lewis with one or two shots that I could tell had shaken him. The champion started to find the range a bit in the sixth and at the end of that round Jerry Roth and Tony Castellano had the fight all square at 57–57, while Adrian Morgan had Bruno well ahead at 59–55. The people's favourite was doing much better than expected.

The seventh followed a similar pattern until Lewis unleashed a concussive left hook that staggered Bruno. Suddenly he had to pay the price for building a career on fighting mugs. He'd never been coached to go down and take a count while he cleared his head. For Frank, you only went down when you were unconscious. That might be brave, but it's very foolish when you are standing opposite a giant of a man with a hurtful punch. Frank just stood there, an easy target. Lewis knew he'd got him and could finish him off, but he tried to make it easier for himself by holding Bruno's head with one hand while winging in punches with the other. I dived in and the crowd thought I'd stopped it. But you can't stop a fight on a foul.

I took Lewis to a neutral corner to give him a lecture and allow Frank to clear his head a bit. But Frank didn't have a fighter's instincts, or the experience of digging deep when it really hurts. He'd never had to find a way to just get through a crisis. As soon as I told them to box on, Lewis was all over him and I quickly got between them to call a halt. The seventh round had lasted just one minute and ten seconds.

By the time I got back to my hotel it was half past four in the morning but people were still crowding round, watching a rerun of the fight on the big screen. When it reached my lecture, the whole room went quiet and looked across at me. One or two started to rib me and for months afterwards, whenever I met Mickey Duff he'd say, 'Don't fuck with me.' I was unrepentant. It may not sound pleasant on television but that's not what I'm about. You can't control two giant men who have worked up real feeling against each other by treating them like naughty boys. The ring is our factory floor and if the TV people want to put microphones in to add to the realism, they've got to accept the way it is, warts and all.

A lot of people clearly didn't agree and I was given some stick in the media about my industrial language. John Morris phoned me from the Board of Control and said: 'Mickey, you were out of order.' I explained why I'd done it, and also told him that I didn't realise there were any mikes there, especially as Mike Goodall had made a point of putting the hand-held microphone close to me when I was giving my final instructions. To try and take the heat out of the situation, I wrote the Board a letter of apology but it didn't appease them and soon after I was invited to appear in front of the disciplinary committee chaired by Sir David Hopkin, the Board's president at the time. He was a nice old boy, the chief Metropolitan magistrate in London, who has sadly passed away since. He had a dry sense of humour and reminded me of Mr Pickwick, with his sideburns down to his chin.

I was a bit confused because the disciplinary meetings are usually held on a Wednesday but my letter was dated for a Monday. I thought, 'Blimey, they must be out to get me, they've given themselves a few days extra.' I was nervous but determined to make a strong case for myself. When I arrived on the Monday morning, John Morris said: 'What are you doing here? The hearing's on Wednesday.' There had obviously been a mix-up over the dates and I explained that I had made special arrangements to be there and couldn't possibly come back on Wednesday. John went off to get in touch with Sir David. Eventually he tracked him down on his mobile phone. He was fishing and they must have been biting well because he decided to stay put. 'Give him a bollocking and send him home,' he told John. It was all over in five minutes.

Looking back, that freezing cold night in Cardiff was the best moment of my life. It wasn't the greatest fight I've been involved in, but the event, the atmosphere, the size of the audience in every corner of the world, and the fact that I was refereeing the biggest fight Britain had ever witnessed for the most important title in boxing, made it something that will stay with me for the rest of my life.

FOURTEEN

The Warriors and the Woeful

If Lewis–Bruno was the biggest fight of my career, two others share top of the bill as the best and most exciting.

The first was the European featherweight title in Compiègne between defending champion Jean Marc Renard of Belgium and Farid Benredjib from France. It was the first time I had worked with Benredjib's promoters, the Acaries brothers, Michel and former European champion, Louis. They were tremendously helpful even though they weren't delighted with the final result.

Renard, who once decked Barry McGuigan in a European title fight, had moved down from superfeatherweight but Benredjib was not at all daunted and the two of them went at it from the first bell and never stopped. This was no tippy-tappy stuff – every shot came from the shoulder. In one round they hardly moved, standing toe to toe, slugging it out – they could have fought in a telephone box. The courage was stunning: each man determined not to flinch, two warriors passionately wanting to take the belt, unwilling to allow anything to stop them. There were two judges and me as scoring referee. One of the judges and I gave it to Renard by a round, while the other judge gave it to Benredjib by the same margin. Both fighters were taken off to hospital for the night: Benredjib had a cracked rib and a broken nose, and needed over 30 stitches; Renard broke his hand, had several facial injuries and also needed a lot of stitches.

The cuts created a tricky situation for me with the ringside doctor, a woman who fortunately was a rare member of that species who was able to take advice. She went into Renard's corner and said she wanted to look at his cut. I said: 'OK, but you don't say anything or make any sign until you have also looked at Benredjib's cuts.' As far as I was concerned they were both equally badly damaged, although not bad enough for me to stop it. She nodded and, after looking at both corners, said: 'They are both bad. I will leave it to you.' I'm sure if she'd only looked at Renard she would have stopped the fight, yet in the end it went the distance.

Cuts always look bad but they are seldom as dangerous as they appear. As a ref, you must make sure the blood is not going to seep into the eye and restrict the vision, which is dangerous. Obviously in a run-of-the-mill fight, where there's not much at stake, you might stop the fight earlier to give the lad a chance to heal quickly and be back in the ring earning his living as soon as possible. But in a championship fight you want to give the boxers every opportunity. As long as an injury isn't health-threatening I will always try to let the lad get to the end of a round so his corner has the chance to work on it. Some of those cuts men can work miracles with only Vaseline, adrenalin and pressure. They have just under a minute to do their job, and I get very annoyed when I see a referee go over midway through the break to check things out. I'll sometimes stand a couple of yards away to take a look, but I won't say anything or interfere. You must give the cuts man the chance to do what he's paid for. There's plenty of time for a ref to make a judgement when the fighters come out for the next round.

Renard–Benredjib was a brilliant fight but it was perhaps just eclipsed by the battle between two South Africans, Philip Ndou and Cassius Baloyi, that sold out Carnival City in 2001. It was voted WBU fight of the year and second overall, though several good judges thought it should have been number one everywhere. I've never come across such intensity and courage in the ring.

Ndou was the WBU junior lightweight champion, a fighter, a real scrapper with a big KO punch. He'd only had one defeat and most of his wins were early finishes. Baloyi was WBU world featherweight champion. He was a boxer although he too carried a dig that could stop people. And to add spice to the proceedings, Nick Durandt, Ndou's trainer, used to look after Baloyi. I'd handled both of them before and they'd asked for me as a neutral referee.

South Africa was split down the middle. Everyone wanted to see the

fight and many were locked out. They missed a classic. In the seventh
round Baloyi had his jaw broken. His face ballooned up and I went to
his corner, but they didn't want to pull him out. He was fighting back
and I couldn't stop it. He never winced once, no matter how hard the
punch to his damaged face. It was a magnificent fight that went the full
12 rounds, with Ndou finally coming out on top on points. As I
showered afterwards I couldn't help but reflect on how their courage
put to shame some of our fighters, who want to quit at the slightest
damage.

We shall have to see if Baloyi comes back from that. Benredjib never
did win the title but I still rate him as one hell of a fighter. Another guy
I rate very highly who never got beyond being national champion is
Gary Mason. To my mind he paid a big price for being in the same
stable as the other two major British heavyweights of the time, Frank
Bruno and Horace Notice. The three of them were streets ahead of the
next batch of John Westgarth, Dave Garside and Glenn McCrory, but
sharing a management, they never came up against each other. For
some reason it was Frank who became the popular favourite and was
guided through to the big titles but I always thought Gary would have
taken the other two if they'd come face to face in the ring.

Horace Notice was a big, fit lad who was underrated by many
people, but I don't think he could take a punch like Gary. As for Frank,
I'm not sure he was ever given a chance to find out if he could be a top
fighter. That might seem an odd thing to say about someone who held
one of the world championship belts for a while, but to me Frank only
did the business when things went his way. I can't remember him ever
digging deep into his reserves and coming out on top. He was fed so
many bodies that on those occasions when he found himself in the
trenches, he didn't know how to battle his way out by sheer willpower
and heart. He was masterful against bodies like John Emmen, but even
someone like Bonecrusher Smith, who was on his way down when
they met, made mincemeat of Frank. And he only avoided defeat by
Jumbo Cummins because the big punch that caught him came right at
the end of a round. If that had landed earlier, I'm convinced Frank
wouldn't have known how to see it through.

I like Frank as a person. He's a world champion PR man, but he's not
in the same class as a fighter. In the fight in Cardiff he was doing quite

well and was ahead on points, but as soon as he got into trouble it was all over. In his first fight with Tyson, he staggered the champ with a big shot, but he didn't have the instinct to follow up and finish it off. I think he was more concerned about staying out of trouble. Their second meeting was a farce. Frank had lost it in his mind before he went in the ring. Tyson produced some of his old hand speed and power and Frank just held on. Mills Lane threatened to disqualify him for holding and he would have done him a favour if he had. When Tyson caught him with a big body shot early in the third round it was as good as over. Frank didn't know how to cover up and finally Tyson unleashed an uppercut that almost took him off his feet. He had no idea of how to defend himself and was soon battered until he was sitting on the ropes and Lane stepped in. The round only lasted 50 seconds.

I don't blame Frank – he made a lot of money, became one of the country's most popular personalities, and is probably set up for life. But he wasn't good for boxing. In the end the public get fed up with watching so-called champions demolish a series of no-hopers. What makes boxing great are the titanic contests where fighters from the top two or three in their weight get it on to see who's best. Years ago, rivals like Henry Cooper and Joe Erskine, Chris Finnegan and John Conteh, Freddie Gilroy and Johnny Caldwell, and many others used to go head to head. Now promoters would keep them apart, each hanging on to his version of the title.

The alphabet soup created by the proliferation of governing bodies makes it possible for two, three or even four boxers each to claim he is the best in the world without the inconvenience of having to face the other claimants. It's all down to greed – not necessarily the greed of the fighters – and it will continue as long as the public and television are willing to pay for meaningless 'championship' bouts. You know the kind of fight I mean – Herbie Hide against a washed-up Tony Tucker, Hide versus Willie Fischer, Hide blowing away Damon Reed, an underweight American, in 52 seconds. That's not to demean Herbie Hide; he showed plenty of guts when he took his limited talent into the ring with Riddick Bowe. And of course a manager should feed the odd body to his man along the way – otherwise we bodies wouldn't make a living! – but when they start to match potential champions against mannequins, boxing suffers another huge dent in its reputation and we just can't afford for that to carry on.

The answer is far more complex than just the impossible dream of returning to one governing body. There were times in the 'good old days' when things weren't that great either. For example when Floyd Patterson was heavyweight champion, he'd defend the title about once a year and have a return clause written into every contract in case he lost. That left a lot of good fighters, like Eddie Machen, permanently on the outside while the title stagnated. What we need is a mechanism that ensures the various champions come together in unification fights, so we get genuinely relevant, top-quality fights.

The public would have loved a clash between Bruno and Mason, and my gut feeling is that Gary would have won quite comfortably. He had a great physique, with that little bit of fat cover you need as a heavyweight, while Frank was muscle-bound and awkward. And Gary had courage enough for two men, as I saw close up when I was judge on his European challenge to Lennox Lewis. It was an all-British affair with Larry O'Connell as ref and John Coyle and I as judges. It was a terrific fight, which Lennox won on a stoppage in the fifth when Gary's eye went. It was his only defeat in a 36-fight career. His eye was gruesome. It turned out he'd detached the retina and it must have hurt like hell, but the Jamaican-born giant who fought out of Wandsworth never took a backward step. If the same thing had happened to Lewis, I'm not sure he would have gone on as long and I'm certain Bruno wouldn't. When Larry stopped the fight he had the scores even, while John Coyle and I had Gary ahead.

Another British fighter I have a lot of time for is Chris Eubank, both as a man and a boxer. He too had a few 'iffy' matches against poor opponents, but when it came to the crunch he proved he had a big heart and no little talent. Although his clash with Michael Watson ended tragically, it was a colossal fight with both men giving out and taking tremendous punishment. And Eubank's contests with Nigel Benn are still worth watching again. Benn dished out a lot of solid, hurtful blows in their first meeting, and also had one of the best 'digs' among middleweights, but Eubank absorbed it all and won on a ninth-round stoppage. And even though he was beaten in his two epics with Carl Thompson, Chris showed what a warrior he was, with skill, punching power and a lot of balls. The first meeting especially was a throwback to the great days of boxing, and it was allowed to flow by referee Roy Francis, which underlines what I've said about ex-fighters making the best refs.

Away from the spotlight, Chris is very different from his public image; he's relaxed and great fun to be with. Like any showman, as soon as an audience or the media turns up he puts on his public face. He injected razzmatazz into boxing over here and it put bums on seats, even if many of them were just longing for him to get his come-uppance. The Americans have always had a showbiz element to their fight presentations – Hector Camacho, who entered the ring in leopardskin trunks roaring 'It's macho time' is a prime example – but it was Chris Eubank, with his leaps over the top rope and his outrageous posing, who brought the glitz to our rings and boxing as a whole benefited.

Prince Naseem Hamed took on the Eubank mantle as a showman but I have to say I don't have nearly as much time for him. There is no doubt he's a talented fighter. He moves brilliantly, throws quick-fire punches from anywhere and has a shot that can finish people off. But his attitude leaves a lot to be desired and it's about time he realised there's more to being a champion than just winning fights. Perhaps he will, now that he's been defeated, but somehow I have my doubts. Every beaten fighter wants a rematch, but to beat Marco Antonio Barrera you've got to be able to outfight him. Nas can't change his style and we've seen that Barrera can cope quite comfortably with what he has to offer. But Nas won't believe that and he's probably convinced himself by now that it was a freak result and returned to his arrogant posturing.

I saw that side of him at its worst when I refereed his WBC international superbantamweight defence against Armando Castro in Glasgow. Nas boxed his socks off but I gave him a right bollocking when he knocked the lad down and then stood there taunting him. Castro was an honest fighter who had come to earn a few bob. I've got no time for 'bottlers'; I'll disqualify them and make sure they don't get their money, but this guy wasn't bottling it. He had done his best and it just hadn't been good enough. There was no reason for Hamed to take the piss. I've been in that position myself and I know it takes guts to get into the ring against someone you know will probably outclass you. The sooner Nas learns that opponents deserve his respect, the better. I stopped the bout in the fourth round, which upset the promoter. He'd had a thousand-pound bet it would finish in the first. It nearly did, but as it was a championship fight I wanted to give Castro every chance as long as he was not getting badly hurt. He wobbled towards the end of the first but he was still able to walk towards me, so I let him go on.

Something that really upset me was the way Nas treated his trainer, Brendan Ingle. I don't know the ins and outs of the dispute that made them split up, but one thing I am sure of – it was Brendan who discovered Nas and developed him, so he'd earned any money that came his way. Boxers don't mind paying up 25 per cent early on. When it's just twenty-five quid out of a hundred, it doesn't seem bad. Even two hundred and fifty out of a grand's OK. But once they start earning the big bucks, they baulk at handing over quarter of a million or more. They forget about all the work that's gone in with little reward in the early days.

Hamed's been blessed with a wonderful talent and faced few setbacks on his way to becoming a multi-millionaire. He probably doesn't appreciate that people like Brendan know what it is like to risk all for a fighter he believes in. I remember when another of his stable, Herol Graham, fought Lindell Holmes outdoors at Sheffield United's Bramall Lane ground, Brendan and his wife Alma mortgaged their house to put the fight on. It rained all that week and for a while it looked as though they might lose everything. Fortunately on fight day the sun shone and they were saved, but they could have still been paying off that mortgage now. I don't think Prince Naseem has any idea of how much people put into making a success of boxers like him. I just hope one day he realises.

In some ways Brendan does bring some of his problems on himself, building up his fighters' confidence so much that they start to believe their own publicity, as I realised when I went to Cardiff to referee Nas against Laureano Ramirez in what turned out to be another quick stoppage. Another of Brendan's lads, Clifton Mitchell, was on the undercard fighting James Oyebola for the vacant British heavyweight title. As I arrived I spotted a car with the legend 'Clifton Mitchell,

British Heavyweight Champion' painted down the side. I thought I'd arrived too late for the fight! There must have been some red faces later when Mitchell was knocked out in the fourth round. Come to think of it, if I'd hung around I might have picked up a cheap car.

'Bomber' Graham was a different lad altogether to Nas. He was very talented, but his awkward style meant he was never big box office, and TV shied away from him, so he never made the big bucks. That's why he had to get back in the ring four years after Frank Grant had outmuscled him to take the British title at Elland Road. I was appointed as referee for the comeback fight. Everyone was a bit anxious and Glyn Rhodes, who was in his corner, came to me before it started. Glyn's a diamond but I always say he was the worst fighter I ever refereed. I hated taking his fights because he was so awkward. He also thought he was a bit of a clown and often came close to getting thrown out, although he never quite stepped over the line. I felt he had prospects but wasted them. To my mind he could have been at least a British champion and I think he realises that now, and is working hard to make sure his fighters don't throw away any talent they have. Anyway, he said to me: 'Mickey, if Bomber's getting hurt, pull him out, will you? He means the world to me. I didn't want him to come back but he insisted, and I don't want him to get hurt.' I assured Glyn he had nothing to worry about. In the end Graham beat Terry Ford, a very limited journeyman from the States, on points but I was convinced that Glyn was right. The former European champion had nothing left in the tank.

It just proves how wrong you can be, because after another unconvincing showing against an overawed Craig Joseph, Herol went on to win the WBC international supermiddleweight title, stopping Chris Johnson in eight rounds. I had just refereed Johnson, an American with a big KO record. A lot of dollars had been invested in him and I thought Herol would struggle to last three rounds, but he did a good job. He then went on and defended the belt against Vinny Pazienza. It shows you shouldn't write off people with courage and determination.

Nigel Benn, the Dark Destroyer, once stopped talking to me for 18 months, but I still think he was a great champion. I rate his demolition of Iran Barkley, a man who later went on to win world titles at two

weights and twice beat Thomas Hearns, as one of the greatest seen
from a British boxer abroad. Nigel started to blank me after I was a
judge on his fight with Nicky Piper. He did a great job, stopping Nicky
in the 11th round. But he'd not done as well in the early part of the
fight and I gather he was well pissed off when the scorecards were
published in *Boxing News* and he saw that I had Piper ahead on points.
The other two judges favoured Nigel but I've watched the fight again
since and I'm still convinced I was right. The next time I saw Nigel was
in Las Vegas when Adrian Morgan, Larry O'Connell and I went over for
the WBC convention. I spotted him having breakfast with Henry
Wharton just before they were due to fight for the title and I remember
thinking: 'That's great, that's what makes boxing special.' That night
there was a big dinner with a galaxy of champions including George
Foreman, Evander Holyfield and Marvin Hagler. I used to collect
signed photographs which I kept with my collection of boxing
memorabilia that was on display in my café before I sold it, and seeing
Nigel about three tables away, I went over to him. When I explained
what I wanted, he just said: 'No. Fuck off and ask Nicky Piper.' I was
embarrassed and left, realising I'd been stupid to ask after hearing he'd
been upset by the decision.

Things didn't resolve themselves until the night of Nigel's epic
confrontation with Gerald McClellan at the London arena, which has
been labelled by some critics as the 'Battle of the Century'. I was there
to judge the Mike McCallum–Carl Jones fight, which was on earlier in
the evening, and found a seat that happened to be near Nigel's corner.
I'd seen McClellan a few times and didn't think Nigel had a prayer. The
press were pretty well agreed this was a fight too far for Benn, and one
guy I know bet eighteen thousand quid that McClellan would stop him
inside three rounds. I thought he was on a sure thing and smiled at the
end of the first round when he looked down the row at me and put his
thumb up. Several times during the fight, Benn looked as though he
just couldn't survive the battering he was taking, but like a true
champion, he summoned up all his resources and managed to fight his
way back into it. McClellan finally went down in the tenth and was
counted out. Later he was taken to hospital and had a blood clot
removed from his brain, which sadly left him permanently damaged.
As soon as the fight was over Nigel went over to the press and gave

them an ear-bashing. Then he went back to his corner and called me over. I thought I was in for another mouthful but instead he said: 'Sorry, Mickey.' And a few days later I received an envelope containing a fabulous picture, signed 'Best wishes, Nigel Benn' in gold ink.

The display of boxing memorabilia that I built up while I owned the Ringside Café in Leeds would be the envy of many collectors. As well as a lot of autographed photos of great champions, pride of place goes to one of Tom Collins's Lonsdale Belts that I bought off him. That would have been the number two item if the prize exhibit hadn't ended up in the rubbish tip. At the WBC convention in Seville I bought some boxing gloves and got them signed by a who's who of fighters – Ingemar Johansson, Lennox Lewis, John Tate, Marvin Hagler, Alan Minter, John H. Stracey, John Conteh, Walter McGowan, Maurice Hope, Dennis Andries, Howard Winston and Ken Buchanan – every one of them a world champion. I was going to Argentina as soon as I got home and as there had been a few break-ins in the area, I hid the gloves. It was several weeks later that I remembered to look for them. I scoured the house from top to bottom but there was no sign. Then the penny dropped. I'd wrapped them in a carrier bag and stuffed them in a black plastic rubbish bag, thinking no thief would look there, then without thinking when I got back from Buenos Aires, put the bag out for the dustman. Later I got some gloves signed by Chris Eubank and Henry Wharton, which we raffled for the kids' football team I ran. They raised four hundred pounds and the girl who won them was offered a hundred quid straight away, so I reckon several grand is rotting away somewhere on a Leeds tip.

That Benn–Piper fight highlights one of the constant controversies in boxing – the disputed points decision. Too many people forget the early rounds, making their judgement on an overall feel for the fight, and are usually swayed by a strong finish. But boxing is scored round by round and no matter how impressive Benn was towards the end of the fight, and he was well on top, I couldn't wipe out those early rounds Piper had won, which put him still slightly ahead on my card.

A classic example of this is the night Henry Gibbs decided Joe Bugner had out-pointed Henry Cooper for the British heavyweight crown. Henry was, like Frank Bruno, the people's champion, a man who had earned his place in the British public's hearts and imaginations with a single punch that sent young Cassius Clay crashing on his back. Only the bell and some shenanigans with a glove prevented Cooper pulling off one of the great shock results of all time. The left hand that floored Muhammad Ali ensured Henry would remain a British legend even though when you look at his record, he had a pretty mixed career and was in many ways a cruiserweight who wouldn't have been able to live with modern heavyweights. Of all the British heavyweights of that era, I reckon Joe Erskine was the best. Brian London was a tough street fighter, European champion Dick Richardson was another who gave referees a hard time, and Richard Dunn, who came a bit later, wasn't a great boxer but he had plenty of balls and always looked to make something happen. Bugner was a good technician but his heart never seemed to be in the fight game. He used his technique to try and stay out of trouble and only occasionally, as when Dunn upset him, did he show that killer instinct to finish off an opponent. On paper, Bugner's record looks quite impressive but I've always said that someone like Joe Frazier fought Muhammad Ali while Joe merely survived against him.

I was with Harry Gibbs in Las Vegas in 1993 as a judge on Lennox Lewis's defence against Tony Tucker. He and I went down to breakfast together and found ourselves at a table just across the aisle from Henry Cooper, who was there working for the BBC. When he saw Harry he looked away as though he'd never seen him before in his life. Apparently he was still pissed off about the verdict and the fact that Harry had made the publishers withdraw a chapter in Cooper's book, slagging off his refereeing. I thought it was disgraceful to snub a man who had given an honest decision just because it went against you. It was not at all in keeping with Cooper's carefully maintained public image. I was pleased to read in *Boxing News* that the two of them finally started talking again after 25 years. Apparently someone said they would give a grand to the charity at a fundraiser if they would shake hands and Henry agreed. But it should never have taken that long. I believe that to be recognised as a true champion, you must be humble enough to accept a decision, even if it is not in your favour. You may not like it, you may not agree with it, but you don't spend 25 years ignoring the man who has given his honest and highly experienced judgement, and who knows substantially more about the job than you do. Henry certainly wouldn't be in my list of top British champions.

A similar, though less significant, thing happened to me when I refereed the Commonwealth title fight between Bobby Vanzie and the South African James Armah. Bobby, who comes from Bradford, lost his title on points and was clearly very unhappy at my decision though most people, including the Board, seemed to agree with me. He came to me afterwards to complain, saying: 'As far as I was concerned I was miles in front. I was cruising in the last six rounds.' I replied: 'Well that's your fault. You get paid to fight 12 rounds, you should have fought 12 rounds.' Not long afterwards I was invited to a show at Elland Road and beforehand the promoter, Kevin Spratt, rang to tell me that I was on the top table with John Conteh and one or two other people including Bobby Vanzie. He then added: 'Bobby has asked me to ask you not to talk to him.' I said: 'Fine, it doesn't bother me. I wasn't planning to be his best friend anyway.' That night he totally blanked me, but I really wasn't worried about it. I didn't rate him as a fighter, and now I don't have much of an opinion of him as a person. I refereed Vanzie again for the WBO international title against Yuri Romanov, a 22 year old who had him down five times before I stopped it in the eighth round. It was only his second defeat so I'm not very lucky for Bobby.

Harry Gibbs was one of the great gentlemen of our game and it was very sad when he died in 1999. As in all sports, media coverage is much more intrusive these days than it used to be, with the deficiencies of officials and players coming under such close scrutiny that it's almost impossible to escape unscathed. But I hope that when I eventually retire, my reputation will be as high as Harry's. I have many happy memories of him, especially when we went together to work on a fight for Don King, the promoter who in one way or another has dominated the fight game over the last decade or so and much as it hurts to say it, deservedly so.

The trip got off to a hectic start. My plane from Leeds–Bradford was running late and I knew I only had about ten minutes between landing and taking off, so I had to get the stewardess to radio ahead and ask if they could rush me through security at Heathrow. They were brilliant and I sat down, sweating like in the old days of roadwork, with about a minute to spare. Unfortunately my bags hadn't made such good progress and followed me out 24 hours later.

After we checked into the hotel, Harry said we should go and pay our respects to Don. We found him in a huge Hollywood-style caravan in the hotel car park. We made our way through a formidable private guard of heavies and were ushered into his presence. That electric-shock hairstyle of his is even more daunting in real life than in the pictures. King shook hands with me, then said: 'Sir Harry, how are you?' He chatted on for a few minutes then added: 'It's really nice to see you again, Sir Harry.' As we made our way back to the hotel I said: 'What's all this Sir Harry business?' Harry looked at me and smiled. 'I got the OBE and Don thinks that's the same as a knighthood. He's obviously very impressed, so I'm not going to tell him any different.'

It was a good fight, with Lewis putting Tucker on the deck for the first time in his career. Lennox took the unanimous decision and I was happy with the job I'd done. I was paid with a cheque, which gave me a few problems because it meant I didn't have enough cash to pay for my hotel extras and buy a few presents. But King has plenty of pull in Vegas and arranged for the casino to cash the cheque into dollars. Harry did the same and as we went through the various checks at the airport to fly home, I spotted a cash bureau and decided to switch the cash to sterling. The girl behind the counter took her time and I was getting a bit anxious about missing the flight, so when she finally paid me out in a whole wad of small notes I just stuffed them in my pocket and ran.

The seat next to me was still empty and the steward enquired where Harry was because they didn't want to lose their take-off slot. I said: 'He's on his way but you'll have to wait for him, he's an old codger with gout and can't walk very fast.' When he arrived, Harry said the girl had run short of English money so couldn't change his dollars, adding: 'Have you counted yours?' I heaved it out of my pocket and started to count, gradually realising I was about a grand light. We'd taken off by then but I was all for making the captain turn round so I could get my cash. Harry just laughed and threw a bundle of notes in my lap. He'd spotted it when he'd been at the counter. I still don't know if it was my carelessness or a devious cashier trying to take advantage of my haste.

When we arrived back at Heathrow my keys set off an alarm and

I had to empty my pockets. I started to drag bundles of cash out of each of the side pockets of my jacket, then pulled a whole load more out of the inside pocket. The security guard just stood there open-mouthed. 'Yeah,' I said. 'I've just been to Vegas and had a great time on the tables.'

FIFTEEN

Time after Time

The luck of the draw means you don't get to referee some boxers at all, whereas you are appointed to almost every fight of others. I've been lucky enough to be in charge of nearly all Ricky Hatton's WBU light-welterweight world title fights and I think he certainly has the chance to go right to the top.

There was a stink when one of his opponents, Eamonn Magee, complained because his challenge would be the seventh Hatton title fight I'd refereed. The Irishman used words like 'shambles' and 'scandalous' and said he definitely did 'not want an English referee'. His manager, Mike Callahan, weighed in with: 'As long as Mickey Vann can count to ten in the normal way when Eamonn knocks Ricky down, that's all that matters. As long as he doesn't take ten minutes to get from one to two.'

Since both fighters have the chance to object to officials when the appointment is first made, as far as I was concerned this was all smoke and mirrors from a camp who knew that if Eamonn couldn't knock Ricky out, he had little chance of out-pointing him. They were looking for some kind of advantage, or perhaps an early excuse. As far as I was concerned I had every right to referee Hatton for a seventh time. No one could point to a single incident in the first six where I had leant unfairly towards him.

The fight itself went quite smoothly. Magee had Hatton down in the first round and shook him to his boots in the second, but the Englishman got out of it through clever ringcraft, giving himself time to clear his head. Perhaps that broke Magee's heart; certainly he went into his shell a bit afterwards. He also went into his corner and I twigged he was taking instructions from his trainer. You always get a certain amount of that and usually ignore it, but this was so blatant that I had to warn them. By the time they get into a ring, boxers should know how to fight an opponent.

The best Ricky Hatton fight I've handled was the previous one against Mikhail Krivolapov, who was ranked number four in the world by the WBC. He'd never been stopped but Ricky boxed him to a standstill in the ninth, taking every round on the way.

My 100th world title fight involved Ricky and made the headlines in a big way because I was attacked by his opponent's dad! There was a bit of muttering when I was appointed to referee the bout between Hatton and young Stephen Smith from Hull, but I didn't take any notice. As usual I went into the dressing-room before the fight to go over the instructions and Stephen's dad, Darkie, started to say something about making sure I didn't push his fighter off harder than Hatton when I separated them. I've known Darkie for years, we were boxing at the same time, so I just put it down to nerves and ignored it.

Hatton was on top from the start and early in the second round he knocked Smith to the canvas. I was starting to count when I suddenly became aware of this figure coming into the ring. When I looked round it was Darkie, complaining that I'd allowed Hatton to use his elbow. According to the rules as soon as any corner man enters the ring, you are supposed to disqualify his boxer. But I didn't want to do that. I shouted: 'Darkie, get out of the ring.' If he'd gone I'd have let the fight continue, but he just ignored me and lunged at me instead. He gave me no option – I waved the fight off.

It was a sad end and I don't have the faintest idea what he thought he was doing. Stephen looked completely shocked and I felt really sorry for the lad. I've looked at the fight on video since and am positive that Hatton did not foul him. Stephen did duck low at one stage and might have hit Ricky's elbow then, but there was no deliberate use of the elbow. I think it underlines how wrong it was to change the rule that banned blood relations from being in the corner. I can understand what it feels like to watch your son getting a hammering, but climbing in the ring is no way to sort it out. Darkie handed in his licence and has been banned by the Board, and I understand he and Stephen aren't speaking, which is very sad. Looking back, I am quite happy with how I handled the situation. If someone came at me like that anywhere else, I'd probably have whacked him but I'm pleased I didn't because it wouldn't have done boxing's fragile reputation any good at all.

Hatton is a great prospect, but in my opinion he still has two weaknesses: he lacks a KO punch, which he can probably compensate for by concentrating on his strong body-punching – a cracked rib will stop a fighter as decisively as a good shot on the jaw. More importantly, I think he needs to tighten up on his defence. He's not chinny but he does leave himself a bit too open and I think at the moment that would give him problems against people like Mickey Ward and Kostya Tszyu, although I think he'd stand a good chance against one of the other leading light-welterweights, Zab Judah. One of the fights I'd love to see if Mickey goes up to welterweight would be against Michele Piccirillo. That would be a hell of a fight.

I've also been involved in five of the championship bouts of Frenchman Anaclet Wamba, and one of them brought me face to face with the most hostile crowd I've ever seen.

Wamba is a French cruiserweight. He's an awkward fighter whose level of performance seems to depend almost entirely on the standard of the opposition. A counter-puncher by nature, he seems to need the opponent to come on to him before he can produce his best form. I reffed him first in Paris, against the American former Olympic gold medallist Anthony Maynard. He dropped Maynard in the first and while the American came back a bit, it was a poor fight. Maynard was much more limited than I expected and Wamba sank to that level, although he did enough to win it comfortably on points.

I judged Wamba against Massimilian Duran in a blood bath refereed by Arthur Mercante, and I was referee in a super contest with Adolpho Washington in Monaco. Washington is a tough customer, a really good fighter, who went on to win the IBF cruiserweight title two years later. He brought the best out in Wamba, who rose to the occasion – in the end the judges couldn't separate them.

I also judged his second defence against Duran, and now I was due to referee the bout with the number one challenger, a useful Argentine, Marcelo Dominguez. The fight was staged in Salta, a town at the foot of the Andes in the far north of Argentina. It was December 1994, and to be honest it never occurred to me I might face some ill feeling from the Falklands war. The journey took over 36 hours – I started by going to France to meet up with the rest of the Europeans on the trip: a judge from Italy, Wamba, the Acaries brothers who managed and promoted him, seconds, trainers and sparring partners.

We had an eight-hour stopover in Buenos Aires, just enough time for a shower, a kip and a quick look round before setting off to Salta. It's an attractive, fairly new town with most of the population under 35 years old. For some strange reason there seemed to be noticeably more blind people on the streets than there are elsewhere. We met up with the other judges from America and the Caribbean island of Aruba, and the next morning we four officials set off sightseeing. Vince Delgado, the American judge, spoke Spanish and acted as our interpreter, and the sight of four obvious strangers soon attracted attention as we wandered around the market place. One guy started to chat to Vince, who then introduced the rest of us. The judges from Italy and Aruba got polite smiles and a handshake but when he said, 'This is our referee, Mickey Vann from England', the guy just spat on the ground and walked off. The others thought this was hilarious and despite my pleas to be introduced from somewhere else – you can take patriotism too far – Vince continued to take great pleasure in telling people I was Mickey Vann from England, and I would get another gob on my shoes.

I soon twigged that if this was the reaction I was getting from individuals, I might have a massive problem on my hands when it came to a large fight crowd, especially as they always unfurl the national flag and play the anthem of the referee as well as that of the two boxers. I said to Vince: 'Look, you've got to help me. There's no way they can play "God Save the Queen", much as I love her. Tell them I'm from Holland or Ireland or something.' He gave me a smile that didn't entirely put my mind at rest. 'No problem, Mickey,' he said.

I went to the weigh-in and rules meeting with the two camps. On this occasion the officials were asked to undertake a medical check as well as the fighters. This happens a lot in America and I'd always sailed through, so I didn't give it a second thought as I took off my shirt. But a minute later I was a worried man. 'Your blood pressure is too high, you cannot referee the fight,' the doctor said. At that my blood pressure really went through the roof, and the doctor was in danger of following it. Not take the fight! Was he bloody mad? He obviously read the situation because he told me to sit quietly for a bit; he would take another reading in half an hour. It was down but not enough, so he told me to relax again. Then he started to hit me on either side of my neck. A couple of minutes later he passed me fit to take charge of the fight. I'm still not sure why he started whacking me – it may have been medical or perhaps he didn't like Englishmen. A few years later I was in Nice to referee the European bantamweight title fight between Frenchman Fabian Guillerme and Russian Alex Yagupov when the officials were again given a medical. I passed OK but one of the judges didn't. He was rushed to hospital and not released until just before the fight.

On the night of the Dominguez–Wamba fight I climbed into the ring and decided that the furled flag held by the very attractive woman next to me had rather too much red, white and blue for comfort. And sure enough, as they announced me I heard the dreaded word 'Angleterre', a roll on the drums and the opening of that familiar British anthem, and the Union Jack was unrolled in all its glory. Hardly had the words 'God save . . .' left my lips before the music was drowned out by an eruption of booing and whistling. I tried to stare straight ahead at the TV cameras and make out I was singing, oblivious to all the noise. It wasn't easy because I was aware of drink cans flashing past my head like Exocet missiles. I glanced down and noticed an American judge with a silly grin on his face.

I decided things would calm down once the fight got underway and certainly for the first few rounds the fans seemed to forget there was a loathsome English dog in the ring. Dominguez was doing well and Wamba was far from his best – he was probably distracted by the thought of being hit by a stray missile meant for me. It was a very close fight but towards the end the Argentine started to tire a bit. All that expectation and nervous energy from the early rounds was beginning to take its toll. In the ninth round he spat his gum shield out a couple of times. It's an old trick that buys tiring boxers a bit of a breather because you have to stop the fight, take him back to his corner so the seconds can wash the shield and replace it. At the end of the round I went to Dominguez's corner and insisted the interpreter made it clear that if the gum shield was spat out again, I would take points off him.

Sure enough, halfway through the next round he began to flag once more and out came the shield. I called time out, took him to his corner and got it replaced. Then I marched him to the centre of the ring and indicated to the judges that I was deducting a point. The crowd went ballistic and for the rest of the fight the volume of abuse hurled at me never went below deafening.

It rose by several decibels when the scores were announced. Wamba had retained his title on a majority verdict 116–115, 115–113, 114–114. If he hadn't lost that point, Dominguez would have been world champion. I climbed out of the ring trying to look cool and nonchalant, but I think if someone had tested my blood pressure then I might have been carted off in an ambulance. As it was, my rescue came in the form of a van reversed at speed into the stadium with the back doors open. The judges and I were bundled in and driven off at pace, to the sound of yet more beer cans thudding against the roof and the side. We went out for a meal and a quiet drink that night but I noticed that as we walked along the three of them stayed a couple of paces behind me, just in case I was recognised. I have to say, though, that I've been back to Argentina since and the hospitality and reception I received were first class.

The next time I came across Wamba was in Paris. I was there to referee the WBC lightweight title between Jean-Baptiste Mendy and Lamar Murphy. There was a little bunch of Brits on the trip: John Keane as one of my judges, and Richie Davies over to judge his first world championship fight, the return between Wamba and Dominguez. Richie was the youngest judge of amateur bouts in the world at the age of 17, and two years later became the youngest referee before switching to the professional code when he was just 26.

We went to the weigh-in together. My two guys went through without any trouble, but when Wamba got on the scales he was six pounds over the limit. He was given two hours to get it off, but instead of going away to skip or have a sauna he just sat there shaking his head. At first I thought it was some kind of con, that maybe he had some weights in his trunks and was trying to make the Dominguez camp believe he was struggling to make the weight and would tire late in the fight. But soon it became apparent there was a real battle going on between him and his camp. No matter what anyone said to him, he wouldn't budge and in the end he refused to get back on the scales. He relinquished his title sitting on a chair at the weigh-in. I couldn't understand it. He'd made nine defences and now he was just throwing it all away. I heard later that whereas he was billed out of St Brieuc in Northern France, he was a naturalised Frenchman who had originally been born in the Congo. Apparently he used to go back there between fights, spend his money on good living and put on a lot of weight. This time it seems he just couldn't be bothered to get it off again, though I'm surprised that his management or trainers didn't notice and do more to get him in shape before it reached that stage. As far as I know he hasn't fought since. I came across him at another show in Paris and he seemed quite happy just being one of the crowd. Poor old Richie was really fed up, missing out on his first world title fight. Since then it's happened to him three more times and if you're invited to work on a major championship with him, you wonder if it's worth turning up because it will probably be called off!

I have to say I was very disappointed with Wamba's attitude. You can't say he lacked heart, because he'd shown plenty when he'd fought Washington, but you wonder if he had what it took to be a real champion. It's something that bothers me about a lot of modern boxers. I just wish a few more of them had the same attitude as Dave Charnley. If ever I'd wanted to be like another fighter, it would have been Dave. Nowadays boxers want to watch several videos of their opponent and try to find out every detail, down to the colour of their mother's eyes. But Dave – the Dartford Destroyer – used to just say: 'They want to fight me? Send 'em over.' He used to take them as they came and usually sent them packing.

He was a southpaw, a good boxer and a great fighter. He once trained with Henry Cooper who described him as 'a wicked body puncher. His eyes were like steel. He was so determined.' And boxing commentator Harry Carpenter called Dave 'a midget Marciano who had only once failed to spank a Yank'. That was before Charnley's first fight against world champion Joe Brown. The American was outstanding, holding the crown for six years from 1956. He continued boxing until 1970 when he was 44 years old. It was unlucky for Dave that Brown was from the same era, so he never added the world belt to British, Empire, and European titles he took with such style. He lost the first fight to Brown in Houston on a cut-eye decision in the fifth. The second fight was an epic battle in Earls Court, when Dave was again badly cut, this time on the bridge of his nose. But he fought through to the end and a lot of people disagreed with referee Tommy Little's decision to give it to the American. Larry O'Connell acted as Dave's sparring partner before those two fights and describes him as the 'best fighter I've ever seen'. The pair still live near each other and play golf together. Dave finally got the better of Brown in Manchester but by then he'd lost his title, so the only satisfaction was the revenge and being only the second person to knock out 'Old Bones' in a 118-bout career.

Another British boxer I admired greatly was Howard Winstone, the winner of two Lonsdale Belts outright by the time he was 24. He'd lost the ends of his fingers on one hand, so he had reduced power, but he made up for it with speed and boxing ability. One of the biggest anticlimaxes I can remember in boxing was when Howard came to Leeds. I'd been looking forward to watching him fight Leroy Jeffrey in the Queen's Hall but he got stopped in the second round. Nevertheless, the Welshman was brilliant even in defeat. Leroy put him down and Winstone was obviously groggy so the American swarmed all over him. But such was Howard's ringcraft that only about one in ten shots landed. He couldn't avoid the inevitable stoppage, but it was still a masterful performance. I reckon if you could have put all the best qualities of Winstone and Charnley into one person, you would have had the supreme fighter.

Possibly the best British boxer of his generation, arguably of all time, was Ken Buchanan. He had everything but because his manager Eddie Thomas was linked to the fading empire of Jack Solomons, Ken spent his early years fighting private club shows in front of small audiences. I've mixed feelings about club shows. They do give an opportunity to young fighters just starting out, but many people in the audience are more interested in the comedian than the boxers, have drunk too much by the time the fights start and don't appreciate the courage of the kids they are watching. Clubs also prevent a lot of ordinary fight fans from seeing the emergence of a local boy and make it harder for him to build up a following. That happened to Buchanan. He even won the British title at the National Sporting Club when most fight fans, even in Scotland, hadn't heard much about him. If you look at the old cuttings, only about a dozen people turned up in Glasgow when Ken first returned home with the world title, yet this was a man who won a rare standing ovation at Madison Square Garden. He fought eight times at the Garden, topping the bill with Muhammad Ali on the undercard on one occasion. Even when he lost his crown in a brawl to the uncompromising Roberto Duran, he worried the Panamanian so much he wouldn't agree to a rematch, and later described Buchanan as the hardest puncher he ever faced.

Sadly, Ken finished his career in unlicensed fights after losing a lot of money in a business venture. He's hit hard times but retained his dignity. I remember seeing him at a show in Manchester when no one seemed to recognise him and he couldn't get in. That's no way for a great champion to be treated, and at a time when millions of pounds are being poured into fighters not fit to lace his gloves, I would have thought the sport could have done more to help someone who is among the best ever to climb into a ring.

One man probably deserves to be called the supreme boxer more than any other – Marvellous Marvin Hagler. He is also in my eyes a supreme person. When you look at his record – middleweight champion for seven years, including twelve defences against top opponents – he has every reason to be big-headed, yet he remains approachable and friendly. He still carries himself like a champion. I might be old-fashioned, but I hate to see champions and former champions wandering round like ragamuffins, as Lloyd Honeyghan used to do. Hagler, in contrast, is always immaculate, stylish and a credit to his sport.

I first met him in a hotel in Las Vegas and, in stark contrast to Mills Lane, who was world class only in his own mind, Marvin took time to chat. I came across him again at a WBC convention in Seville. He and I checked in at the same time and once more he was happy to spend time having a chat. When he left, he sought me out to say goodbye. I walked him to his taxi, we said our farewells and as his cab drove off, he turned and waved. It was a small gesture but I can think of many world champions who wouldn't have bothered to make it.

To me Hagler is even more special than Muhammad Ali; if I had to choose the top boxer of all time, I'd vote for him. If it were a question of having to choose to spend time with one or the other, though, I'd find it impossible to decide. There's no taking away Ali's genius as a fighter, nor his outstanding work as an ambassador for the sport. No one else in the world could go absolutely anywhere and be recognised and revered in the way he can, and few moments in sport have been more moving than when he lit the Olympic flame. But he spoiled it at times. I didn't like all that 'What's my name' stuff with Ernie Terrell, and he went on fighting long after he should have quit.

Hagler retired after his controversial defeat by Sugar Ray Leonard. He was still at the top, still to most people the greatest middleweight in the world. He could have come back, and was offered big bucks to do so, but having made the decision he had the willpower to stick to it, even though he admitted he had been tempted. 'I try to stay out of the gym,' he said. 'Once you get the smell and start punching the bag, you're tempted to get back in the ring.'

Although I was a nothing fighter I found it hard to stop, so I realise it must be even harder for those who have been at the top and enjoyed being champions, revered by millions of fans. I spoke to Steve Collins in Belfast after he'd quit and he assured me he would never come back. 'Why would I? I've got a beautiful home, a lovely family, a gym where I work with some boxers and I do a bit of media work. I've enough money for my needs. Why should I start pounding the streets at four in the morning again?' But he couldn't resist the siren call, and eventually tried to return.

Proud fighters hate to admit they are past their best. I refereed Barry McGuigan's last fight against Jim McDonnell, and Barry was very upset when I stopped it on a cut eye. The 'Clones Cyclone' was a true fighter, the kind you have to nail to the floor before he will admit he is beaten. He'd been a wonderful champion – no one who saw that amazing win over the gallant Eusebio Pedroza at Queens Park Rangers' football ground will ever forget it – but he'd suffered in his defence in the searing Nevada heat against Steve Cruz, taken a hammer blow when his father died, and the split from his manager Barney Eastwood had also taken its toll.

McGuigan won his first two comeback fights without really impressing, and he never got going against McDonnell at the G-Mex Centre in Manchester. He lost every round and was badly cut in the second. I always tell a corner that if they can do a job on a cut and it's not dangerous to the boxer, he can carry on. Some of the cuts men, like Denny Mancini, Danny Holland and Paddy Byrne, who was in McGuigan's corner for most of his big fights, can do miracles, and can make the difference between defeat and victory. This time Barry had Ernie Fossey in his corner, another artist with cuts, but even he couldn't do anything with this one and I called it off early in the fourth. Barry was clearly upset at the time and had a go at me, but he couldn't see the cut himself and didn't realise how bad it was. Later he apologised in the press for his outburst. Unlike Henry Cooper, he took a second look at the situation, without rose-tinted glasses, and wrote in his autobiography: 'Vann was right, it was a nasty cut, lying open.'

SIXTEEN

Alphabet Soup and Hungry Fighters

Barry McGuigan was part of a golden era of British boxing, a time when there were many top-rate, charismatic fighters around. We still have a lot of boxers in this country but the standard has gone down. It's partly down to the fact that the coaches are not as good as the old-style guys and partly because the amateur scene, where most boxers get their start, is weak.

Amateur boxing is still shot through with well-meaning but incompetent people, who teach kids things like the necessity of keeping their heads up and not ducking. Why the hell not? Ducking is one of the best ways of avoiding getting punched. If you go too low, you can leave yourself off balance and vulnerable, but the art of coaching involves teaching them to duck properly, not just forbidding it outright. It doesn't help that boxing is now banned from schools but I doubt we are ever going to reverse that bit of politically correct nonsense. I read recently that one school is so afraid of being sued if a kid gets injured that they have switched from rugby to football, so boxing has no chance. There's also a daft idea that kids shouldn't be made to compete because they get upset if they lose. If we carry on like this there will be no sport in schools at all, and we will end up with a generation of losers.

I'm sad to say there are not many young fighters coming through in this country at the moment; perhaps there are fewer hungry kids. One problem is that there isn't the scope for a youngster to learn his trade and build up a following. Young guys are turning pro with hardly any amateur bouts under their belt. Anyone who shows a bit of promise is rushed through the system, often against bodies, and is fighting for the British title after about ten fights. It might sound like a tired old plea for the 'good old days', but the difference then was that by the time a fighter got to challenge for a title, he knew his way around. There's a big danger now that if you haven't 'made it' after 15 to 20 fights, the promoters write you off. It's strange to think that Marvin Hagler had 60 fights before he challenged for the world title. I think that made him a better fighter and a greater champion.

Part of the blame must lie with the media, who seem to believe the only fights worth reporting or showing on TV are title fights. I'm not sure the public agrees with that. When I visit some of the smaller halls that somehow manage to survive against the odds, the punters seem to be more concerned with a good scrap than whether or not it's for a meaningless title. I don't understand why the press can't follow the rise of a few fighters – the setbacks as well as the wins – as they slowly build towards a confrontation with the current champion and, eventually, with each other. After all, they don't just report on the FA Cup final – they cover all the rounds up to it, the triumphs, the disappointments and the unknowns who find sudden fame. It provides interesting reading and great TV, so why don't they do the same with boxing?

I remember the way rivalry was built up between Frankie 'The Tiger' Taylor and Lennie 'The Lion' Williams towards their inevitable confrontation. The public became so caught up in it that the featherweight pair were paid the then considerable sum of a thousand pounds for a six-round contest with no title at stake. Frankie was a gutsy little fighter, who made a good living out of the fight game and went on to write about it in a newspaper column when he hung up his gloves. I thought it was dreadful when he turned round and bit the hand that had been feeding him for years by saying boxing should be banned.

At the moment in this country, only Ricky Hatton and Joe Calzaghe can be certain of having a chance to go right to the top. There are a few kids coming through – and a lot of Asian kids joining the amateur ranks – but we still don't know how good they will become. I've judged a couple of Calzaghe fights: the first was against David Starie, and it stank the place out. If I'd been inside the ring I think I might have disqualified both of them. But I was also at ringside when Calzaghe fought Omar Sheika. He was brilliant that night; he pulled all the stops out.

The one British fighter who is unquestionably world-class is of course Lennox Lewis. I wasn't surprised, or particularly impressed, when he stopped Mike Tyson because 'Iron Mike' was well past his formidable best. But I think he might well have taken Tyson even when Tyson was at the top of his power. Bonecrusher Smith was a bit like Lewis but not so good. He could box and had his head screwed on, and when he got his chance for the title, he fiddled and mucked Tyson around for 11 rounds then outboxed him in the 12th. If Tyson couldn't get people out early, he ran out of ideas. If you could ignore his awesome power and his intimidating stature and reputation, you had a chance. Lennox can box; he has a punch, and he also has the brains to know how to overcome opponents.

I rate Lennox in the top three or four of all time, behind Ali and Joe Frazier. He would have been tested more if he'd have been around at the time of boxers like Ernie Shavers, George Foreman and Frazier, but he has produced some impressive performances against fighters like Tommy Morrison and Ray Mercer. He did a good job stopping Andrew Golota in the first round, and Tony Tucker was still a good fighter when Lennox became the first opponent to put him on the canvas. People talk about fighters like Rocky Marciano, but you have to remember he was really only a light heavyweight. The guys now are four or five stones heavier and Lennox would have taken him out without too much trouble.

The heavyweight scene always commands the most interest and I'm afraid that apart from Lennox, it's not looking too clever at the moment. Wladimir Klitshko, the Ukranian WBO champion, is probably the best of the rest and there's a guy in America, Baby Joe Mesi, who looks a decent prospect. I also have a soft spot for South African heavyweight Corrie Sanders even though he came unstuck against Hasim Rahman. Sanders, who also plays rugby, had a damaged knee that later required an operation and should have pulled out of the fight. Nevertheless he knocked Rahman down twice, and round six of the fight was voted the best single round of the year. I still think Sanders has great potential. That was only his second defeat in over 30 fights. He's as big as Lennox Lewis and I think he could go on and do just as well, but I have little time for other so-called contenders, like Chris Byrd. They could only be a danger to Lewis if he went to sleep in a fight with them, like he did against Rahman.

I'm afraid Audley Harrison just doesn't have enough time on his side to make it to the top. Around the age of 30, he should be in his prime, not starting to learn his professional trade. I may be proved wrong, but I think his best hope is the British title which, sadly, doesn't mean much around the world these days.

Audley was right to turn pro and cash in after winning his Olympic gold medal, but I do think that if he'd been serious about getting among the really top fighters, he would have switched to the pro ranks several years before, when he was in his early 20s. Because the heavyweights always get so much attention he was guaranteed a high profile straight away, but his first few fights were far from impressive. I think he would have had a better chance if he'd signed up with someone like Frank Warren, who is without doubt the best promoter and manager in Britain. Frank would have handled things differently. Because of his age, Audley is in a hurry and he can't afford to have his promoters making mistakes and going through the learning process at the same time as he is.

Part of the problem of knowing where fighters stand in relation to each other is the completely nonsensical way the ratings are done. One of the reasons I joined up with the WBU in 1996 – apart from the fact that I know I'm going to get plenty of work – is that they are the only governing body who have an objective ranking which includes fighters from other organisations. There's no suggestion that you can use influence or money to get your fighter up the rankings as there is with some organisations. Anyone who believes the rankings are kosher should remember that IBF president, Bobby Lee, was jailed after a long trial for just such shenanigans.

It's a complete nonsense that Lennox Lewis doesn't appear in some heavyweight rankings when he's clearly the best around. And there are plenty of other examples. Jorge Barrios from Argentina was pretty well universally ranked around sixth in the world when he knocked out Silvana Usini from Italy in the seventh round to win the vacant WBU superfeatherweight belt. Immediately he was dropped from the other rankings. He hadn't done anything wrong. He'd just followed his profession as well as he knew how and become, at that time, the only world champion Argentina had. That's the extent of the politics in the fight game and it stinks. A fighter's job is to fight, the same as a bricklayer's job is to lay bricks. It doesn't matter if he builds a Safeway supermarket one week and an Asda one the next. Just because the two are competitors doesn't make him any less a brickie.

One of the current crop of fighters I have a lot of time for is Michele Piccirillo from Italy, who has signed up with Don King. He's a cracking fighter. I telephoned *Boxing News* when he was going to fight British champion Geoff McCreesh for the vacant European belt, but they wouldn't believe me when I said Piccirillo would win. In the event he outfought McCreesh and stopped him in the ninth round. Geoff's manager Jim Evans, someone I rate very highly, said to me: 'If they had still been fighting, Geoff wouldn't have beaten him.' I refereed Piccirillo against the outstanding Argentine southpaw Juan Martin Coggi, a former WBA champion, who has an impressive record with only 4 defeats in over 80 fights. The Italian won on points by some distance. I think he could beat De La Hoya.

Boxing is still a sport where 'hungry' fighters can claw their way to fame and fortune, which is why a country like Mexico with its extreme poverty is producing so many champions. I think the same is going to apply to some of the Middle Eastern states and Africa, and the first two could be the Matumla brothers from Tanzania. I reffed Rashid in Vincenza against Paolo Pizzmaiglio. He's super cool and has a 'goodnight Vienna' punch. The Italian crowd had waited months for this fight and were noisily behind their man, but you could have heard a pin drop when Matumla knocked him sparko. The lad got up but didn't have a clue where he was. He could have done with Aussie Rod Carr's second in his corner. Carr was knocked out of the ring in Leeds by Henry Wharton and landed just near me. When he got back in through the ropes the bell rang and Carr slumped on his stool. I heard him ask his second 'Where am I?' to which came the quick reply: 'You're in Melbourne, mate. Can't you hear them cheering for you?'

Matumla's brother Mbwana, a lightning-quick bantamweight, was with him in Italy. He'd come to fight another local lad but when he pulled out, Mbwana agreed to fight an exhibition against a bantamweight. The kid knew no fear and was immediately slugging it out with the bigger guy. It became a bit of a war and the ref had to step in and remind them it was only an exhibition and they should calm down. The pair of them still have some way to go, but they are certainly worth watching out for.

SEVENTEEN

Death of a Master Showman

The saddest period of my life was in the mid-'90s. In 18 months, I lost the person I loved most in the world, my dad, and Karen, my girlfriend of eight and a half years, dumped me.

For years my dad had lived at Garforth House, a mansion near Leeds with a glass-domed, parquet-floored ballroom, six bedrooms, three bathrooms and a wine cellar. Dad still lived in his caravan, of course. He made a living from running a children's zoo in the grounds and kept a lioness named Lisa in the house, and a flock of geese outside instead of a guard dog.

He and Olga had a son, my little brother Carl, who is in his mid-30s, about a year younger than my eldest son, Tony. Eventually they divorced and Olga moved into the converted stable block at Garforth House, where she still lives. They sold the rest of the house and some of the grounds, and Dad phoned me to say he was buying a block of lock-up garages in Armley Town Street in Leeds and was going to move his caravan in there. It was one of the frequent coincidences that crop up in my life; I had recently sold those garages to Steve Sykes, so I was able to ring him up and get the price down a bit. He made a profit but didn't rip off my dad. Strangely enough, Steve's sister Sarah was later to move in with Tony and have a child with him, William, one of my grandsons.

Dad moved his caravan into one of the garages and lived there. He had running water and used to have an electric fire, which he turned on its back so he could put his frying pan on it. It was a bit primitive but he never saw it like that. He was at home in a wagon. It was what he was used to and what he wanted. He used another of the garages as a workshop where he made theatrical and fairground sideshows. He put an advert in *World's Fair* and sold them to make a bob or two. He also produced illusions and sold some of them to Paul Daniels. I had my skip business at the time and Dad would come into the yard and sort through the rubbish for some decent timber, metal brackets, half cans of paint, screws or anything else he could recycle. He was against being wasteful and spending money unnecessarily.

He was around 80 by then, although he certainly didn't look it. He was still upright and sprightly, and could get away with telling TV companies he was 60. He kept an old Honda Civic in another of the garages and used to charge the battery up every two or three weeks so he could use it to drive to Manchester to work for Granada, or up to Esholt when he had a part as an extra in *Emmerdale*. He'd never passed a driving test in his life and although his eyesight was by that time very dodgy, somehow he got around OK. His sight had never been that great, even when he was throwing knives, and when I was about 13 we were driving in his Jag through Leeds when the police stopped him because he was swerving all over the road. They thought he was drunk but in reality he was having problems seeing where he was going. I ran home and told Olga, who went to get him out of jail while I took the spare keys and collected the car. I'd been used to driving lorries round the circus so it wasn't a problem, and I was helped by the fact that Dad had fitted blocks on the pedals for Olga, who is only 5 ft 2 in. tall.

Dad was an independent old cuss but he and I were at last talking again. We would chat on the phone from time to time, although if he called and you were out, he wouldn't ring back. And he seldom rang late at night, so I was a bit surprised to get a call as I made myself a cup of coffee after arriving home from my trip to Monaco to referee Wamba and Washington. It was after midnight and when he said he wasn't feeling too good, I shot straight round there. I'm no Florence Nightingale but I am a great believer in the benefits of a nip of brandy. It stems from a family story about the birth of Uncle George. Legend has it that the doctor took one look at the lifeless body of the new baby and declared there was nothing he could do to help him. As he left, he gave my grandma tuppence for the other kids. She immediately sent one of them out to buy a tot of brandy off a neighbour, then spent the night wetting the baby's lips with it. George came round and lived to be 84.

When I reached the caravan Dad was in bed, complaining of pains in his chest. He didn't have any brandy so I knocked up a pal of mine, Dave Hardcastle, who shrugged off the unearthly hour and gave me a bottle out of his cupboard. I poured Dad a shot in a cup of coffee and it seemed to make him feel a bit better. I settled down on the floor and told him about the fight, about the hotel and seeing Boris Becker and Ringo Starr. Eventually we dozed off, but after a while I became aware Dad was feeling poorly again. I'd never seen him like that and decided he needed to see someone who knew a bit more than me. He didn't have a doctor so I rang for an ambulance. They wouldn't come out when I gave the address as a block of garages so I manhandled him into my car and drove him to Leeds General Infirmary, where they immediately rushed him into the cardiac department. He'd had a heart attack.

I didn't sleep much that night but when I got to the hospital the next day Dad was sitting up and looking fine, despite the pipes and wires that were attached to him. The doctors said they wanted to keep him in for observation and tests, which he grumbled about but accepted. I went to see him every day. He seemed to be getting better and by Friday was back to his cantankerous best, grumbling when they said they were keeping him in until the following Monday. 'I'm not staying here another weekend with these old codgers,' he said to me. 'Bring me my clothes tomorrow. I'm going home.' Dad had a thing about illness and hospitals and had once told me that if he ever got so ill he wasn't able to look after himself, he'd put a hose on his car exhaust and commit suicide. I'd heard that's a painful death, so I bought him a large bottle of tablets and a bottle of whisky to wash them down, and I told him that, if necessary, I would feed them to him rather than have him put in a nursing home. I felt as that was his wish, it was my duty as his son to help him any way I could.

I argued that if the doctors recommended he stay a couple more days, he should, but they finally agreed to discharge him the following day. We sat there chatting for about three hours and suddenly all the things I'd wanted to say to him poured out of me. I still don't know why it happened. The Van Normans don't discuss feelings. They just get on with it. Karen had persuaded me to express my emotions a bit more but it still seemed strange, especially with Dad. I said: 'Dad, I've always wanted you to be proud of me but I never seemed to be able to do anything that really pleased you,' and reminded him of an incident that still hurt me when I thought of it 40 years later. Dad always said people who listen at doors never hear good of themselves and that was certainly true when I listened to him on the phone to uncle Tom, who had obviously rung to ask if I could help out on his shows. I heard Dad say: 'You don't want Mike. He always walks about with his head in the clouds. He'll never make anything of himself.' That hit me harder than any punch I took in the ring – my own dad thought I was a waste of space.

I also reminded him that he'd never been to see me box, neither as an amateur when I was on the fringe of the England team, nor as a pro 'doing it for real' as he would say. He hadn't been to see me referee until I took him to a Henry Wharton fight in Leeds several years after I started. Once he got there, of course, he was immediately the centre of attention. He was still a flamboyant figure with his ponytail, still charismatic, and all my mates thought he was great. I felt very proud of him, but as I had told him that night in the LGI, I wished he'd come because he was interested in what I was doing and not just because I'd insisted on picking him up.

All the hurtful things he'd done to me poured out that night. I wasn't angry; I just wanted to make him understand how I felt about him and how I'd hoped he would feel about me. I was always aware as a kid how much he'd achieved and it burned me up every time he told me I wouldn't amount to much. I'd do anything I could to try and please him, even searching the roadside as I walked around to try and find some nuts, bolts or washers he would think were useful. I just wanted to hear him say: 'Well done, Mike.'

As he sat in hospital, listening to my outburst, Dad was clearly surprised and muttered that he'd never realised and had been busy when I was growing up, which was about as close to an admission of regret as I was going to get. I put my arm round him and gave him a big hug, something I'd never done before. 'You get some rest,' I said. 'You look great. I'll pick you up in the morning after I've been to the café. I love you, Dad.' He hated anything like that, but I felt really good and closer to him than I'd ever been. He waved me away and shouted something he often used to say to me as a kid: 'Take your hands out of your pockets – put them in someone else's.' I smiled – he was obviously feeling better.

I was just finishing serving breakfasts at the café the next morning when I got a call from the hospital asking me to go there straight away. My immediate thought was that the old bugger was playing up so I said: 'Tell him to behave himself. I'll be there as soon as I've finished here.' The nurse replied: 'No, Mr Norman. Please come now.'

When I reached the ward the curtains were pulled round his bed but I still didn't twig, until the nurse took me into a side room and told me Dad had died that morning. He'd had another heart attack. I was numb. How could my dad be dead? He'd never been ill before. It hadn't occurred to me he could die in hospital with all those people and expensive machines to look after him. I pulled aside the curtains and looked at him. Someone had put a daffodil on his chest. He looked wonderful, calm and strong. I sat beside his bed and cried. I talked to him for a long time; I don't know what about, but it was as if I was chatting to one of my mates. He just lay there as though he was listening to me.

There was little about Dad that the experts would pick out as an example of how to be the perfect parent. Some of those experts might point to the shortcomings in my own life and blame the way I was brought up. But I am so proud to be the son of Hal Denver, one of the greatest showmen of his generation. I'm pleased that I'd just got in when he'd phoned because if I hadn't answered, he wouldn't have phoned again and might have died alone in the caravan in a lock-up. And I'm especially grateful that despite any ducking and diving I've done in my life, someone up there looked down on me and allowed me that last night when we were able to talk like never before.

We had scarcely spoken about death but when we went to Uncle George's funeral a few months before, I'd asked Dad where he was going to be buried and he'd told me there was a space for him next to his mother and father in Croydon. I wasn't sure how to go about things and had visions of having to put the coffin on a truck and take it down to the station to go south, and I was relieved when the funeral directors told me they would take care of everything.

We gave him a great send-off. He would have loved it. We took him

from Aunty Brenda's in a horse-drawn hearse just as we had Uncle
Arthur, and there was a good turnout to see him on his way. I was so
keen to make sure everything went well that I didn't feel any emotion
until they lowered the coffin into the ground. It was so final. Dad was
gone.

There's one more space left in the family grave and people asked me
if that was where I'd be buried. I told them no. I'm the middle son and
a Leeds lad now. I'll probably end up near Ma at Lawnswood. Maybe
Monty will be buried next to Dad. He lives nearby in Coulsdon. We get
on OK now, though we're still not close. Before Dad's funeral I'd never
been to his home or met his family. Probably if Dad was given a choice
about who would spend eternity next to him, he'd pick Carl. He went
with Olga after the divorce and became a photographer, travelling all
over the world on cruiseliners. But I've got the feeling he was the one
Dad cared about most. He used to talk about 'My son, Carl' but never
'My son, Monty' or 'My son, Mike'. But none of that matters any more.
I reckon I was the luckiest of the three sons in many ways because I
got to spend those years with him when he was at the peak of his fame.
I think I probably knew the real Hal Denver better than the other two.
And maybe he cared about me more than he ever let on, because when
I was sorting out his things, I found scrapbooks with cuttings about
my career.

Dad's death knocked the stuffing out of me and things got even
bleaker when Karen dumped me. She had become a very important
part of my life and I thought we had a relationship that would endure,
despite the difference in our ages and the difficult circumstances.

Her husband had become suspicious and hired a private detective,
who obviously soon found out about me and reported back. I was
driving along Whitehall Road in Leeds one day when I saw Karen's
husband coming the other way. As I checked my mirror I saw him do
a U-turn and start to follow me, so I pulled over. He got out of his car
and started to shout at me. He was a big Iranian, about 16 or 17 stone,
but I was mad about the way he'd been treating Karen and was ready
to take him on. We went round the back of the houses and I smacked
him a couple of times, bloodying his nose, and he ripped my shirt. It
was something and nothing, but I knew he'd go straight back and give
Karen hell so I phoned and told her to get out.

Her divorce dragged on for some time and much as I tried to ignore my fears, I could sense things were changing between us. I was hoping that when it was all over we would set up home together. I heard later that she had told her friends at work she was going to marry me, but perhaps I'd outlasted my usefulness. Whatever the reason, that Christmas Karen told me it was all over; she loved me, but wasn't in love with me. That was the KO punch. The relationship was over and I vowed I would never again get into a position where I could be hurt that deeply.

Like Mickey Rooney said: 'I buy women shoes and they use them to walk away from me.' Maybe it's because I'm not a great believer in all this women's liberation stuff. I think we should get back to the old days when there was a clear difference between the sexes, and when men treated women like ladies. I think the male of the species is still the one who is expected to take responsibility when things go wrong. He is capable of working harder physically and should be prepared to be the protector and to put everything on the line for his partner – that's why men usually die younger. But it's not enough for modern women. They want equality as well. Of course their opinions matter, but if you can't work things out by discussion, the male should have the final say.

For me the ultimate folly of the liberation movement is women's boxing. I can see absolutely no merit in it or justification for it. I believe it should be banned. I have no grudges against women – they are wonderful creatures and have an important part to play in life, especially as wives and mothers. They even have a place in boxing – but not in the ring. There are many sports women can compete in that are far more suited to their physical makeup. Apart from the freak aspect of seeing females fighting, there is not much to attract spectators. Most women boxers are very limited in their ability. There will always be exceptions but Jane Couch, Britain's most famous woman boxer is not one of them. All she is doing is causing incredible problems for a great sport. I find it strange that this woman, who believes so much in her ability and supposedly loves boxing, should take the governing body to court and risk bankrupting the sport. As I guessed when she started out, she soon wanted to fight against men. She's already challenged me in the letters column of *Boxing News*. If she hangs around until I'm 65 and retired, I'd be glad to oblige her. The

BBBC is highly regarded round the world and has done a hell of a lot towards making boxing safer. It still has a lot to do and can ill afford to waste money on tinpot court cases like that.

If women want to fight and believe people want to watch them, let them set up their own governing body and stage their own promotions. Surely that is what equality is about? Women golfers and tennis players have done that, and even though they have some top-class athletes, they find it difficult to attract crowds, TV and sponsorship. The public recognises that men are faster, stronger, more competitive and more entertaining than women, and the rewards are therefore greater. I believe women's boxing would struggle even more than golf and tennis to attract a following and they probably know it. That's why they are trying to ride on the backs of the men's game. They are not wanted and have been forced upon us by a ridiculous legal system that's frightened of upsetting the women's lobby. This could have a catastrophic effect on boxing. What will happen if a woman is seriously injured or even killed in the ring? There is always an outcry and calls for the sport to be banned when it happens to a man, but if it ever happens to a woman the sport will do well to survive the uproar that follows.

Several women do a superb job in the administration of boxing, better than some of their male counterparts. I bow to no one in my admiration for Enza Jaccoponi, the general secretary of the European Boxing Union; Patricia, who works with Sauland, the top promoter in Germany; Natalie who is a vital part of the Acaries organisation in France; Anne-Marie, who is a freelance publicist; Shona, who works for Rodney Berman of South Africa; and Jan, with Frank Warren's company Sports Network. And it's not just in administration that women shine. Tanya Follett is a licensed trainer, second and manager and does a good job, and Alma Ingle may be less well known than her husband Brendan, but she is an excellent promoter.

I still have plenty of time for women and love their company. I've now been in a relationship for a while, with a delightful lady from Leeds, Marie Proctor, and it seems to be working out. But perhaps I should take Dave Parris's advice. When he heard that Karen had left, he said: 'Mickey, you should get a nice pensioner with one leg – then she can't run away from you.'

EIGHTEEN

I'm Still Hoping for the Cathedral

As always when I'm in the trenches, it was boxing that brought me through that dark phase of my life and I guess it will be until the day they drag me kicking and screaming from the ring, and force me to hang up my bow tie, and put away my patent-leather shoes and Union Jack socks.

I've indicated in this book that there are things in the sport I would like to change, but overall I'm delighted that so much of my life has taken place inside the square ring. Refereeing has brought me the fame I craved as a kid. As with everything in life, there's been a price to pay. My marriage might have had a better chance if I'd not followed Tommy Miller's advice to become a ref. And of course there are always newspapers that take great pleasure in trying to drag down people in the public eye.

I experienced that when the *News of the World* ran a story that I was selling drugs from my café in Leeds. It came about because one of the girls who worked there was talking to some workmen about her weekend and confessed she had been smoking a joint. I wasn't there at the time, but apparently one of the guys then sold her some grass. About a week later he returned with two other men, who turned out to be reporters from the paper, and this time they tried to buy some from her. She agreed to meet them at her house but when they arrived they said they didn't have enough money and asked if she could take it down to the café the next day. Unfortunately for me she did. I wasn't aware of what was going on, but as far as the *News of the Screws* was concerned, that was enough for them to brand my café as a den of iniquity with me as the biggest villain.

The fact that the police looked at their so-called evidence, including a video, and took no further action against me or the girl counts for little in the eyes of the media. Nor does the fact that the BBBC went through everything in detail and interviewed me, finding no case to answer. In cuttings files around the world for the rest of time, I am branded a drug dealer. I find it disgusting that people can go around trying to trap others just to sell a few more copies of a grubby little newspaper. Sadly, it seems to be becoming more and more the way they operate, and these days whenever I hear a story about victims like rugby player Lawrence Dallaglio, disc jockey Johnny Walker, and Jack Straw's son, my first instinct is to believe it's a fit up.

I know I'm no saint. I've done my share of dodgy things but no more than the average guy, which is really what I am. I just happen to have been lucky enough to be good at something that has put me in the spotlight and made me better known than some of the other people in my street. Boxing's been my life and even though I'm now in my 50s, I still have some ambitions left to fulfil. By the time I retire, I would like to have refereed in Madison Square Garden, the cathedral of boxing. The Garden is known throughout the world and instantly brings to mind some of the greatest fights the sport has ever seen. I nearly made it there when I was appointed to take Angel Manfreddy for the WBU featherweight championship, but the New York Boxing Commission refused me, saying one of their own referees had to take the fight. They also insisted on one of their own judges being appointed. The same thing happened for the Lewis–Holyfield fight and look what we got from Eugene Williams, the New York judge, another woman trying to take over in a man's world and falling short. This closed-shop policy is also practised in Nevada and some other states where they seem to think nobody does it better than their own guys. They'll forgive me for having my doubts.

At some time I would like to be recognised as the best referee in the world. Dad couldn't fail to be proud then, and what a shot in the arm it would be for British officials. I remember how proud I felt when John Coyle was voted number one.

I want to remain happy and healthy like Dad, only for 20 years longer. I always remember people wishing each other health, wealth and happiness at Christmas. Health and happiness are all you need. If you've got those, you've got wealth.

Karen rang me a couple of times since but she's the past. I no longer regret the way things turned out. Rita and I meet occasionally with the grandchildren. She had a hell of a lot to put up with from me, and it's nice that we still don't talk! Olga and I chat from time to time on the phone, and she's been a great help with some of the early memories for this book, but I have no contact with Ella, my biological mother. Aunty Brenda put us in touch after a gap of 27 years and Ella came to see me. She was living in Streatham and I started to write her long letters telling her all the family news and about her grandchildren. I'd write about ten pages but her replies were about ten lines, so I thought she wasn't bothered and stopped writing. She phoned one day and said: 'If you don't want to write to me, don't bother. It's all right with me.' I said 'OK,' and slammed the phone down. We've not been in touch since. She now lives in a nursing home for showbiz people. I don't know if I'll go and see her before she dies. Maybe.

But it's been a great life so far. I was married for 25 years, I've been an amateur and professional sportsman, and I've had my share of women friends – probably not my fair share but there's still life in this chauvinistic bastard. I've made a reasonably good living. I've had a building company, a mobile greengrocers, a repair garage with my father-in-law, a car sales company, a roofing company, two cafés, a skip hire company and a business erecting portable buildings. When I got into that I wanted people to know I was around so I put up a sign saying 'If you want it putting up, call Vann erections'. It got changed to 'Vann erectors' by public demand.

The important thing for me is that I've had immense enjoyment from everything I've done. There have been occasions when I've not necessarily looked forward to what I had to do the next day, but I've never had a bad day at the office. There's always been something round the corner. Like everyone else, I've had bills I couldn't afford to pay, but before you knew it, I'd had a good week at the café or the Board called me with a job, or Jon Robinson asked me to go abroad and take a fight.

I have two sons, Tony and Gary, whom I'm very proud of. They are both in relationships and I hope they work harder at them than I did.

Tony, who works for the Post Office, was a tough lad. He was an amateur rugby league player and had the chance to sign for Hunslet under coach Peter Jarvis, but preferred to stay amateur. Gary was a sprinter and hurdler for Leeds City and won a silver medal at Gateshead and a bronze at Crystal Palace in the Dunlop junior championships. Then he turned to a job as a dance DJ and worked with M People and at Back to Basics, which was club of the year on several occasions. I used to see his name on posters and on more than one occasion, I've been asked if I'm Gary Norman's dad and could I get his autograph. Neither of them showed any interest in boxing – they probably remember the state I used to come home in when they were boys. Tony gave me a grandson, William, and from Gary I have a granddaughter, Libby and a grandson, Benjamin. The grandchildren find it much easier to get round me than the boys did when they were small.

There are times when I think about leaving England because I believe the place is losing its values. Money seems to be the only thing that counts now. It's become the only way to measure someone's worth and I just don't see the world that way. I sold my café and bought a place in Spain with the thought of living over there but now I've met Marie I have more reason to stay here. Who knows? Maybe it's time to take Shirley Parris's advice to settle down, take the plunge again and buy her a wedding ring. Certainly I hope there will be many more rings for me to referee in. Whatever happens and wherever I end up, I'm sure it will be exciting and I will enjoy it. If you're in the area – give me a ring.

The End